THE LIBERATION OF THE EARTH

Dwight Dunbar

ISBN 979-8-89043-886-7 (paperback)
ISBN 979-8-89043-887-4 (digital)

Copyright © 2023 by Dwight Dunbar

All rights reserved. No part of this publication may be reproduced, distributed, or transmitted in any form or by any means, including photocopying, recording, or other electronic or mechanical methods without the prior written permission of the publisher. For permission requests, solicit the publisher via the address below.

Christian Faith Publishing
832 Park Avenue
Meadville, PA 16335
www.christianfaithpublishing.com

Printed in the United States of America

CONTENTS

The Liberation of the Earth

We are living in the greatest days of the church of Jesus Christ. The Bible says, all of creation is waiting for the revealing of the sons of God. This is happening right now. No longer will the body of Jesus on the earth be intimidated and silent. Isaiah 60 says, "Arise, shine your light has come! And the glory of the Lord is risen upon you. For behold, the darkness shall cover the earth, and deep darkness the people; But the Lord will arise over you, And His glory will be seen upon you."

In Jesus was life, and the life was the light of men. Ever since the resurrection of Jesus Christ from the dead, that eternal life and light has come into the mortal bodies of all who believe that He is the Son of God. As the light of God becomes stronger through people getting saved out of darkness and the revealing of the sons of God, the darkness is being exposed and destroyed.

There is one God. There is no other. Jesus said, "My Father and I are one." He told Phillip, "If you have seen

Me, you have seen the Father." That same Spirit that rose from the dead and defeated the devil now dwells in you. You are the sons of God. You are more than conquerors. You are kings and priests on the earth.

We are the kingdom of God. There is a righteous government on the earth right now and has been expanding for two thousand years. Every other government will bow to the kingdom of God on earth. Rejoice in the Lord always. Again, I say, rejoice! The earth is the Lord's and the fullness thereof. You will see the knowledge of the glory of the Lord cover the earth as the waters cover the sea. The best is yet to come.

Hallelujah!

CHAPTER 1

In the Beginning

In the beginning, God created the heavens and the earth. In the beginning was the Word, and the Word was with God, and the Word was God. He was in the beginning with God. All things were made through Him, and without Him, nothing was made that was made. In Him was life, and the life was the light of men. And the light shines in the darkness, and the darkness did not comprehend or overcome it.

The earth was not always without form and void and darkness on the face of the deep. The Word says, "God is light, and in Him is no darkness at all." Jesus said, "I saw Satan fall like lightning from heaven." Jesus was still the Word in heaven when he saw Satan fall. Isaiah 14:12–15 says, "How you are fallen from heaven, O Lucifer, son of the morning! How you are cut down to the ground, you who weakened the nations! For you said in your heart: 'I will ascend into heaven, I will exalt my throne above the stars of God; I will also sit on the mount of the congregation on the farthest sides of the north; I will ascend above the heights of the clouds, I will be like the Most High.' Yet you shall be brought down to Sheol, to the lowest depths of the Pit."

The condition of the earth in Genesis 1:2 is a result of that judgment. Lucifer was one of the most powerful angels. But rather than serving the only true God, he tried to take His place. Jesus said in Mark 12:29, "The first of all the commandments is: 'Hear, O Israel, the Lord our God, the Lord is one.'" There is one God. The evil one disobeyed the main command and truth and received eternal judgment. In Jude 6, it says that "the angels who did not keep their proper domain, but left their own abode, He has reserved in everlasting chains under darkness for the judgement of the great day." The fallen angels are chained in darkness until the judgment when they will be cast into the lake of fire (the second death).

The Spirit of God, hovering over the face of the waters, is the reclaiming of the earth from that judgment of darkness. The earth is the Lord's and the fullness thereof. The devil has never owned anything. He was a servant of the only true God, but he was never an owner.

God is going to reassign dominion and stewardship of the earth not to angels but now to man. God said, "Let

Us make man in Our image, according to Our likeness; let them have dominion over the fish of the sea, over the birds of the air, and over the cattle, over all the earth." So the Lord God formed man of the dust of the ground and breathed into his nostrils the breath of life; and man became a living being.

The Lord God planted a garden eastward in Eden and put the man there.

God made trees to grow for beauty and for food. The tree of life was in the midst of the garden and the tree of the knowledge of good and evil. The Lord God told the man that he could eat of every tree in the garden but not to eat of the tree of the knowledge of good and evil, for if you do, on that day you will die. God had not yet pulled Eve out of the body of Adam. The command was given to Adam.

Prior to Eve eating of the tree of the knowledge of good and evil, the devil and darkness were on the earth, but Adam and Eve were totally unaware and unaffected. They operated fully in the grace and favor and light of Almighty God. It was heaven on earth for them. Adam had dominion over everything on earth. There was no death, no lack, and no disease. The joy of the Lord God was their strength.

Adam neglected his authority over Eve as God gave him the command not to eat of the tree of the knowledge of good and evil. If you put God first place in your life, then you will obey Him. If you put God first place, then you believe God. Faith is basically taking God at His Word. The enemy will always tempt you to compromise God as first love and priority. Seek first the kingdom of God, and He will meet all your needs. If Adam had honored God as his first love, he would have rebuked Eve sternly for even talking with the snake. Adam had dominion; he could have crushed the devil's head. God is a God of order, and the devil is a fallen angel of chaos and disorder.

Eve was deceived by the devil and ate of the tree of the knowledge of good and evil. Adam was not deceived, but not only did he not stand in his place but ate, even knowing the consequences of his action.

The word tree in the *Greek Strong's* 6095 is a tree (its firmness). But the root word is 6095, which means to fasten. Now Adam and Eve had been fastened to the tree of the knowledge of good and evil. Now the father of lies had deceived Eve and Adam, who knowingly participated, and they were fastened to the tree. The devil, chained under everlasting darkness, pulled all of mankind into a world of death and darkness and sickness and poverty. Since man was given dominion over every living thing created prior to the creation of Adam, every living thing under Adam's dominion began to die as well. The devil that was outside man now was in their midst. All of creation on earth sank into darkness and death once again. It says in Romans 8:20, "Because the creation was subjected to futility, not willingly, but because of Him who subjected it in hope." Because Adam and Eve received death in their midst, everything on earth under their jurisdiction had to take on death as well.

Adam and Eve died in the spirit the day they ate of the tree of knowledge of good and evil. Adam's fleshly body would live under the sway of the evil one for over nine hundred years. They were birthed into death because they did not believe God but rather believed a lie.

God was not pleased, but He was not defeated. God can never ever be defeated. The Lord God prophesied to the serpent, the devil, that day; the Seed (Jesus Christ) of a woman shall bruise (crush) your head of your seed, and you shall bruise His heel. The angel, chained under darkness, had assumed dominion in the earth realm, but the Lord God said, "There is a better day coming, and Man will once again rule the earth."

As for Adam and Eve, God said, "We must remove them from the garden before they eat of the tree of life and remain in the realm of the dead forever." They are now fastened to the tree of the knowledge of good and evil. The Lord said, "They will not have to remain there forever. I will hang on a tree and set them free."

I want to end each chapter with some decrees. The Bible says, "The testimony of Jesus is the spirit of prophesy." The Lord God sees the end from the beginning. Darkness has had its day. The light has come, and the kingdom of God is advancing like never before. God is raising a fearless church that is ready and able to govern the earth forever.

- Do not fear in this hour, for the wrath of God will not touch you.
- I will not suffer my church to wrath.
- Rejoice in the Lord always. Again I say, rejoice!
- You are divinely protected, and no evil shall befall you.
- Only believe God.
- Always believe God.

CHAPTER 2

The Blessing on a Nation

God so loved the world He gave His only begotten Son that whoever believes in Him shall not perish but have everlasting life.

—John 3:16

God loves the human race. God loves people. God loves you. In order to enter and remain in the love of God, we must believe Him. The devil is still roaming around like a roaring lion, seeking whom he may devour. But because you choose to believe God, the devil cannot touch you.

The enemy's power is in deception. He is a liar from the beginning. Man was given dominion over the earth and every created thing in it. The devil always uses idols to put something between God and man. "You shall have no other gods before Me." An idol is a false god. There is only one true God, who is the Father of our Lord Jesus Christ. The first idol used against man was the tree of the knowledge of good and evil. God's word was, "Do not eat of it, or you will surely die." The devil mispresented the tree as a way to be like God, and Eve believed the lie. Adam was the son of God, but he was not God. Eve believed the devil, and Adam disobeyed God. Adam's first idol was Eve. Now all future generations sank into the midst of darkness, death, poverty, perversion, and chaos.

In spite of the curse of sin and death in the flesh, there were still men who chose to believe and serve God. Enoch was one of those men. Enoch did not even see a physical death.

And Enoch walked with God; and he was not, for God took him. (Genesis 5:24)

In Hebrews 11, it says, "By faith Noah, being divinely warned of things not yet seen, moved with godly fear, prepared an ark for the saving of his household, by which he condemned the world and became heir of the righteousness which is according to faith." Faith is simply believing God and taking Him at His word. Noah was not a perfect man in the flesh but was righteous because he believed God and did what He said concerning the ark.

The Spirit of God was on certain men who believed Him even after the fall or the sinking of mankind into everlasting darkness. The Lord wanted to put His Spirit back on a nation. The world was exceedingly dark and evil. In the midst of this dark time, God calls out His nation to represent Him on earth.

> **Now the Lord had said to Abram: "Get out of your country, from your family and from your father's house, to a land that I will show you. I will make you a great nation; I will bless you and make your name great; and you shall be a blessing. I will bless those who bless you, and I will curse him who curses you; and in you all the families of the earth shall be blessed." So Abram departed as the Lord had spoken to him, and Lot went with him. And Abram was seventy-five years old when he departed from Haran. (Genesis 12:1–4)**

God told Abram, "If you believe and obey me, I will make you a great nation." Abram believed God and, at seventy-five years old, obeyed God and left his family and country. "Get away from all the false gods and idols and follow Me, and I will make your name great and all the nations of the earth shall be blessed because of your faith." Praise God. Now the Spirit of the Lord rest upon a nation.

God's Spirit did rest upon Abram, and God's blessing was apparent.

Abram was very rich in livestock, in silver, and in gold. God's blessing will eventually show up in the visible for anyone who chooses to obey Him.

Abram was very blessed and wealthy, but at age eighty-five, he still did not have children to be the heir of his great wealth or, more importantly, to fulfill the promise of future prosperity to his bloodline.

When Abram was ninety-nine years old, the Lord appeared to him and said, "I am Almighty God. Walk before me and be blameless. And I will make My covenant between Me and you and will multiply you exceedingly." God said, "My part of the covenant is that I will make you the father of many nations. Now it won't be just one nation I will bless but many. I will change your name from Abram (exalted father) to Abraham (father of many nations). I will make you exceedingly fruitful, and I will make nations of you, and kings shall come from you (King David and Jesus Christ). It will be an everlasting covenant after you throughout all generations. I will give you all the land of Canaan as an everlasting possession. I will be their God."

Abraham's part of the covenant was that every male child would be circumcised. That is Abraham's sign that he accepted the covenant with Almighty God. Abraham believed God and circumcised all the males in his house that very day. No one had ever been circumcised before. But that same day, Abraham believed God and obeyed God. That is faith. Abraham believed God, and it was accounted to him as righteousness. Faith is to hear God, believe God, and obey God. Then God performs the supernatural. Abraham was ninety-nine years old. He did not consider the deadness of his body. He could no longer produce a natural seed. He did not consider that Sarah's womb was dead. He did believe the Word of God. What is impossible with men is possible with God. God took the dead body of Abraham and the dead womb of Sarah, and by their faith in His promise, He produced a supernatural seed, Isaac. Praise the name of the Most High God.

God is the God of Abraham, Isaac, and Jacob. Jacob would later wrestle with God for his blessing, and God changed his name from Jacob (deceiver) to Israel (Prince with God). God now identifies as the God of Israel. God's Spirit rests upon the nation of Israel.

The natural bloodline of Abraham was the covenant people of God until Messiah. Messiah brought a better covenant with better promises. Jesus Christ is Messiah. He is the new creation. He is the firstborn of the dead. God so loved the world He gave His only begotten Son that whoever believes in Him shall not perish but have everlasting life. The Jews who rejected Jesus as Messiah were broken off the new covenant. The Jews who believed Jesus as the Son of God were grafted into the tree of life. The Jews who did not believe Jesus as the Son of God were broken off because of unbelief. The church of Jesus Christ now became God's covenant people. Through the Jews came the oracles of God.

Romans 11:25–28 says, "For I do not desire you should be ignorant of this mystery, lest you should be wise in your own opinion, that blindness in part happened to Israel until the fullness of the Gentiles has come in. And so all Israel will be saved, as it is written. 'The Deliverer will come out of Zion, and He will turn away ungodliness from Jacob; for this is My covenant with them, when I take away their sins.'" Concerning the gospel, they are enemies for your sake. But concerning the election, they are beloved for the sake of the fathers.

God's blessing now does not just rest on one nation but many nations, as was prophesied to Abraham. For by grace, you have been saved through faith and not of yourselves; it is the gift of God. Whosoever will, let him come and drink of the waters of life freely. The new covenant circumcision is a circumcision of the heart made in the Spirit by faith in Jesus Christ as Messiah.

The ground rules for seeing the miracle power of God produce in your life have not changed. If you believe God and then obey Him, He will perform things that are not naturally possible to happen.

When I was praying about planting a church in 1999, I was serving in two churches as a part-time pastor. I prayed, "Lord, I don't care what I do, but I want to know your will." I was praying one evening in my living room at home, standing with my hands in the air, and the phone rang. I answered, and it was a man I had met several years before when he was at a Baptist Church in our town. He was from Africa, and we went out and prayed while he was here on several occasions. He said, "Dwight, this is Manny. What time is it there?"

I said, "It is 5:40 p.m."

He said, "I am in Durban, South Africa. It is 12:40 in the morning. The Lord told me to call you. I told Him I would call you in the morning. He said, 'Call him now.' The Lord told me to tell you that you are to start a work. Does that make sense to you?"

I said, "Yes, I was standing with my hands in the air, praying about that."

He said, "Thank you. Good night."

I heard from the Lord, but I still had to obey. The name of the church we planted is Work of God.

- God is raising a people in this hour, whose faith cannot be shaken.
- Taste and see that the Lord is good.
- I have made you to be more than conquerors.
- Greater is He who is in you than he that is in the world.
- Rejoice, for you were born for such a time as this.
- Thy kingdom come, Thy will be done on earth as it is in heaven.
- The earth is the Lord's and the fullness thereof.

CHAPTER 3

The Promise and the Law

The law of Moses was given by God for the forgiveness of sins through the shedding of innocent blood. The law of Moses provided the blotting out of sins for Israel one time each year. The promise of Abraham was given by God not to forgive sin but to receive supernatural empowerment to accomplish the impossible. They are two completely different issues. One is for the forgiveness of sins and release from the power of the evil one. One is to operate in the class of God.

The first five books of the Bible were told to Moses by God. Moses recorded them as God spoke to him. God gave Moses all the exact details for the tabernacle and how it was to be built, including the specific lengths and materials. In the same way, God spoke the first five books of the Bible to Moses, and he wrote what He said. All scripture is prophetic. Scripture means Holy Writ. Writ means legal authority, like a summons or a subpoena. God is not a respecter of persons. If you believe any scripture of God, it has legal authority to come to pass in your life. I got saved in 1979. My brother and I started a restaurant in 1987. I believed the prophetic Scripture in Deuteronomy 28.8: "The Lord will command the blessing on you in your store-houses and in all to which you set your hand, and He will bless you in the land which the Lord is giving you." The franchise did not want to approve the restaurant because they had no stores in a market as small as ours. There are only about five thousand people in our town. Finally, they approved the site. For the next thirty-five years, that store did twice the national average sales of that chain every year. God's word is prophetic. If you believe, God will always keep His part of the covenant. Praise the name of Jesus. God is not a respecter of persons, but He can only reward those who believe Him. It is impossible to please God without faith, for he who comes to God must believe He is, and He is a rewarder of those who diligently seek Him. Faith in His living Word is the key to exploits and rewards. God wants you to prosper. Through faith, I have been grafted into the tree of life, Jesus Christ. The old and new covenant scriptures are prophetic to me by faith. I am one with God in the Spirit of Jesus Christ.

There are some people who get offended when you say God wants to prosper them. But poverty is a curse and came as a result of the fall of Adam and Eve. The assigned managers of the earth and all its wealth sank into poverty and slavery. There is a lot of talk these days about who the first slaves were and where it did start. The first slaves were Adam and Eve, and it started in the garden of Eden. The devil was the first slave master and remains so until this day for anyone not born again in God.

Beloved, I pray that you may prosper in all things and be in health, just as your soul prospers. (3 John 2)

God died to deliver you from the environment of the evil one. That environment includes darkness, poverty, death, sickness, greed, pride, and fear. Jesus said, "I have come that you might have life and more abundantly."

My dad left my mom when I was ten years old. There were five of us children still at home, ranging from a junior in high school to a four-year-old. Mom had never worked before Dad left. Dad never came back and rarely paid child support. We were challenged economically. One of my brothers and I were only fifteen months apart in age. Mom was very disorganized after Dad left, and I understand why she was. I was about twelve, and I asked Mom if I was a mistake. She said, "You were all mistakes." Well, hallelujah (I think). It does not matter where you are or what condition you are in, if you start walking with God, you will prosper. There is a covenant of wealth to those who obey His financial instructions. Obey the promise of tithing, and experience the supernatural provision of wealth. If anyone struggles with God's blessing of wealth, I pray that spirit of poverty is broken off you now in the name of Jesus.

The legal requirement for the transfer of God's promise to you is faith. In order to take delivery, you must believe God's promise. Abraham's miracle to be able to produce a child at ninety-nine years old was solely his faith that God would keep His promise. He was fully convinced that God would do what He promised. Faith is to obey God in order to see the promise of God fulfilled. Isaac was the proof of Abraham's faith in the promise of God.

The law to Moses came 430 years later, but it was never a replacement or competitor to the promise of God. The law was given to show Israel its sins. The promise of God is that "if you will believe My word, you will experience miraculous results. I will perform it," says the Lord.

Now to Abraham and his Seed were the promises made. He does not say, "And to seeds," as of many, but as of one, "And to your Seed," who is Christ. And

this I say, that the law, which was four hundred and thirty years later, cannot annul the covenant that was confirmed before God in Christ, that it should make the promise of no effect. For if the inheritance is of the law, it is no longer of promise; but God gave it to Abraham by promise. What purpose does the law serve? It was added because of transgressions, till the Seed should come to whom the promise was made. (Galatians 3:16–19)

The law will never produce supernatural results. The law was given to identify sin. I would not have known covetousness unless the law had said, "You shall not covet." The law is holy, and the commandment was holy and just and good. The law was spiritual. But man did not yet have dominion over the earth again. We were sold under sin. Dominion of the earth was still under fallen angels. The law was given to define sin (transgressions) and to forgive sin one time each year. The high priest of Israel would go into the most holy place in the tabernacle and sacrifice a lamb without spot or wrinkle, and the blood would forgive Israel's sins for one more year. The law was a temporary cancellation of the sin of God's people until the promised Seed came. The law was for the identification and removal of sin on a yearly basis from Israel until the promise came.

The promise by God was that He would send the Lamb of God, and He would be sacrificed one time for all the sins of the world and that whoever believes in Him will have all their sins forgiven, not for one year, but forever. "Not only that, but I will send the Spirit of the Seed back into the hearts of the believers, and they will no longer be under the law of sin and death." The promise is by faith. You are sinless by faith in the blood of Jesus. You are now under the law of the Spirit of life in Christ Jesus. Your sins have been removed as far as the east is from the west. Not only are your sins forgiven, but you have become sons of God through faith in Christ Jesus. God has sent forth the Spirit of His Son into your heart, crying out, "Father, Father!"

I thank God for my Father. I am a son of God by the seed of Jesus Christ. I was able to lead my dad to the Lord in the hospital in Indianapolis a few months before he died. His wife called and said, "If you want to see your dad, you better come now." I drove up. I said, "Dad, are you good to meet the Lord?"

He had a tracheal tube in his throat, but he was whispering, "Too bad, too bad."

I said, "Dad, nobody is too bad. Jesus died for all of our sins."

He received Jesus as Savior that night. I always loved Dad. I look forward to seeing him again. He is my brother now. We have the same Father.

Decrees

- God is good, and His mercy endures forever.
- I decree people who feel unworthy to know how much God loves them.
- I loved you enough that I died for you, and I died as you.
- I did not come to condemn you but to save you.
- What can wash away my sin? Nothing but the blood of Jesus.

CHAPTER 4

One God Becomes Flesh

In the beginning was the Word, and the Word was with God, and the Word was God. He was in the beginning with God. All things were made through Him, and without Him nothing was made that was made. In Him was life, and the life was the light of men. And the light shines in the darkness, and the darkness did not comprehend it.

And the Word became flesh and dwelt among us, and we behold His glory, the glory as of the only begotten of the Father, full of grace and truth.

—John 1:1–5, 14

The Word was God, and now God has become a Man, and the Father would name Him Jesus, for He will save His people from their sins.

God did not have to become a man. He did not have to die for the sins of man. He could have destroyed the devil and all the fallen angels in a twinkling of an eye. He could have given all men what they deserved under the law. He could have destroyed all mankind, and the Word would still be God. For all have sinned and fallen short of the glory of God.

God is love. In this, the love of God was manifested toward us that God has sent His only begotten Son into the world that we might live through Him. In this is love, not that we loved God, but that He loved us and sent His Son to be the atonement for our sins. Atonement means to make reparations for wrongdoing. God is love, but God is also righteous. He was the wronged party, and there was no one who could pay for the reparations. There was none righteous—no, not one. But God so loved the world that He gave His only begotten Son that whosoever believes in Him will not perish but have everlasting life.

You hear a lot about reparations these days. The whites did the blacks wrong. Reparations should be paid. The Native Indians (can I still say Indians) in this country were done wrong, and they deserve reparations. I remember when the veterans of the Vietnam War came home, and they were spit on and mocked at the airports. Reparations should be paid. Did all these things happen? Was there wrongdoing? Were there lynchings? Yes. Was it wrong? Yes. Did the US government drive the Indians forcibly off their land (the trail of tears) and kill those who resisted? Yes. It was not the Spirit of God who did this. God loves people. God became a human being. It is the spirit of the devil behind all these acts. The thief has come to steal, kill, and destroy. The devil loves to set people against people to kill people. It was the fallen angels acting out in people behind all the wrongs mentioned above. It was the spirit of antichrist. I pray that people's eyes are opened and the thief is exposed and destroyed so that true reparations can be paid from heaven. I grew up listening to Crosby, Stills & Nash, Jackson Browne, and Marvin Gaye. Their protest songs were always about the Man. The man they were singing about—and didn't know it—were the men knowingly being controlled by the fallen angels. It is a group of men and women knowingly punishing innocent people for power and control and self-gain. Collectively on earth, at any given time, this is the man of sin.

It is the WHO and the WEF and the Bilderberg, to name a few. It is the antichrist spirit operating through men of all color and race and nationality. Decree the light of God over them in the name of Jesus.

Back to the reparations for God. God was the wronged party, and there was not one to pay the reparations.

> **And another angel came out from the altar, who had power over fire, and he cried with a loud cry to him who had the sharp sickle, saying, "Thrust in your sharp sickle and gather the clusters of the vine of the earth, for her grapes are fully ripe." So the angel thrust his sickle into the earth, and threw it into the great winepress of the wrath of God. And the winepress was trampled outside the city, and blood came out of the winepress, up to the horses' bridles, for one thousand six hundred furlongs. (Revelation 14:18–20)**

It was God that was wronged. Men made in His image were bowing down to false gods. It was God who deserved reparations. But there was no one to appease his wrath. So God became Man to pay the reparations. The Word became flesh. Jesus said, "I am the true vine."

> **Why is Your apparel red, and Your garments like one who treads in the wine-**

press? "I have trodden them in My anger, and trampled them in My fury; their blood is sprinkled upon My garments, and I have stained all My robes. For the day of vengeance is in My heart, and the year of My redeemed has come. I looked, but there was no one to help, and I wondered that there was no one to uphold; therefore My own arm brought salvation for Me; and My own fury, it sustained Me. I have trodden down the peoples in My anger, made them drunk in My fury, and brought down their strength to the earth." (Isaiah 63:2–6)

The blood that John and Isaiah saw was in the Spirit. In the Spirit revelation of the blood of Jesus, it looked like 184 miles long and to a horse's bridle. The blood shed by Jesus on the cross was enough to pay the Father reparations for every person's sin that ever lived. "This is My Son in whom I am well pleased." God's wrath is satisfied concerning His people.

And being found in the appearance as a man, He humbled Himself and

became obedient to the point of death, even the death of the cross. Therefore God also has highly exalted Him and given Him a name which is above every name, that at the name of Jesus every knee should bow, of those in heaven, and those on earth, and of those under the earth, and that every tongue should confess that Jesus Christ is Lord, to the glory of God the Father. (Philippians 2:8–11)

I got saved in 1979. I was twenty-four years old. For the next fifteen years, when I prayed, I would always pray to Jesus. One day, I was driving from Mitchell to Bedford. We had stores in both towns. The towns were about ten miles apart. I was praying like I always did, and the Lord said, "Why don't you ever pray to the Father?"

I said, "I don't know. I don't have a problem with it."

He said, "Go ahead and do it then."

I said, "Father," and I started crying so hard that I could not drive, and I had to pull off the highway. I cried so hard for about ten minutes that my body was heaving, and I was making these deep bellowing sounds. The love of the Father overwhelmed me that day. I had never felt anything like it in my life. I was completely undone. I forgave my dad that day.

The love that the Word had for the Father is amazing that He would become Man. The love that Jesus had for the Father was amazing that He would pay the reparations for the wrath of the Father. Jesus was willing to die to fulfill the Father's desire. The Father was heaving and bellowing. For three hours, the sun would not shine, the earth shook, and the rocks split. The veil in the temple was torn in two. Jesus' body was the veil that was rent.

The door in heaven was opened. Now we can go boldly to the throne room in heaven. It is done. Jesus and Father are one again. They are in you. "We will never leave you or forsake you. We love you with an everlasting love, a love greater than death." He was clothed with a robe dipped in blood, and His Name is called the Word of God.

Decrees

- Perfect love casts out all fear. God's love for you is perfect.
- You are the head and not the tail.
- You are the new creation; old things have passed away.
- God is for you, and God is in you.

- If God did not spare His own Son, will He not freely give you all things?
- Say "God loves me" three times.

CHAPTER 5

The Kingdom of God

When God the Word became a man, He came preaching the kingdom of God. Matthew 4:17 says, "From that time Jesus began to preach and to say, 'Repent for the kingdom of heaven is at hand.'" The word *repent* means "to think differently." The liberation of the earth is at hand. The power of the Most High God is coming on a people. The promise of Abraham is here. Think differently. "The power of the devil is going to be destroyed by My death and resurrection. I am starting a new creation of human beings. I am starting a new creation of people, who will have all authority over the powers of darkness and the devil himself. You will no longer be slaves. But now, by faith in Jesus Christ, you will be kings and priests on the earth." The law of the Spirit of life in Christ Jesus has made me free from the law of sin and death.

When Jesus was asked by His disciples how they should pray, He did not tell them to pray that they should immediately be taken to heaven. No! He said, "Pray this way: Your kingdom come. Your will be done on earth as it is in heaven." Your kingdom come on earth, on earth, on earth as it is in heaven. The kingdom of heaven came on the Day of Pentecost and has expanded on earth ever since. Hallelujah!

When Jesus died on the tree, He cried out, "It is finished." The Father's plan to buy back the human race and the earth was complete. Man was once again given dominion over the earth. You were not purchased with gold or silver or perishable things but with the precious blood of Jesus Christ, the Lamb of God.

And Jesus came and spoke to them, saying, "All authority has been given to Me in heaven and on earth." (Matthew 28:18)

All authority means all authority. But we are born again of the Spirit of God. Our flesh, our bodies, are not redeemed. We have the Spirit of the resurrected Jesus in our bodies, but our bodies are not glorified. Jesus' body is glorified, and He is the firstborn from the dead. Our bodies continue to age and die. When Jesus comes in His glorified body, then we who are alive and remain will receive our glorified bodies, like His glorified body.

Our warfare to defeat our enemies on earth is a spiritual warfare. It is a faith fight. Do we believe God's report of the victory of the Man, Jesus Christ? Flesh and blood are not our enemy. People are not our enemies. We fight against principalities, against powers, against the rulers of darkness of this age, against spirit wickedness in the heavenlies (fallen angels).

Now when He was asked by the Pharisees when the kingdom of God would come, He answered them and said, "The kingdom of God does not come with observation, nor will they say, 'See here!' or 'See there!' For the kingdom of God is within you." (Luke 17:20–21)

The Spirit of God is like the wind. You cannot see the wind. You can see the effects of the wind, but you cannot see the wind. On April 3, 1974, I was at Hanover College in Indiana. At 3:50 p.m., a tornado came through the campus. I went down into the basement of Wiley Hall for about fifteen minutes as the storm passed. When I came out of the dormitory, all the trees and most of the buildings were gone. The effects of the wind were obvious. When someone gets saved, they don't look any different with the natural eye. But in the midst of that person, the Spirit of the resurrected Jesus has invaded them. The person that was born from their mother's womb died with Jesus on the cross. The God of all creation has set up permanent residence within that person. They are a new creation, people with the Spirit of God inside their mortal bodies.

The disciples had witnessed Jesus performing so many miracles. He had raised the dead, healed the sick, and cast out devils. They had witnessed Jesus die on the tree. They saw Him put in the tomb. Now they are talking to Him after He was raised from the dead. They were certainly believers. But He told them to go to Jerusalem and wait until they were endued with power from on high. They believed Jesus had risen from the dead, and they were talking with Him. But He said, "You need power."

It is the baptism of the Spirit of Jesus that provides the power to remove mountains in a believer's life. It is the baptism of the Spirit of Jesus that gives you power over demons. Demons are fallen angels, operating through human bodies. Baptism in the Spirit raises you to operate above the angels. God never intended you to be saved and weak. Baptism means to be whelmed. The Spirit of Jesus overwhelms you. It is Jesus Christ in you, the hope of glory. If you are a Christian, and you have never done so, ask the Father to fill you, to overwhelm you with the Spirit of Jesus. Receive it by faith in the name of Jesus.

The cessation doctrine is a teaching in the church that all spiritual gifts—like baptism of the Holy Spirit, healing, tongues, and prophecy—ceased with the original apostles. I believe the cessation teaching and the rapture teaching are the two main reasons the enemies of Jesus have not been made His footstool. If the body of Jesus believes miracles have ceased, how will we make Jesus' enemies His footstool?

For the kingdom of God is not in word but in power. (1 Corinthians 4:20)

I believe you can be saved but not filled with the Holy Spirit. One of the best Christians I ever knew was not filled with the Holy Spirit. He said that he made a vow to the church he served in that if he ever spoke in tongues that he would resign. But the power of the miraculous comes with the baptism of the Holy Spirit. Tarry in Jerusalem until you are endued with power from on high. I lived twelve years as a Christian without the baptism of Holy Spirit. It is a powerless Christian life.

He who believes in Me, as the Scripture has said, out of His heart will flow rivers

of living waters. But this He spoke concerning the Spirit, whom those believing in Him would receive; for the Holy Spirit was not yet given, because Jesus was not yet glorified. (John 7:38–39)

Jesus did not do any miracles for thirty years. Then He was baptized with the Spirit and performed miracles until His sacrifice. He died to forgive sin, but He also died to empower His body (church) with the same Spirit that raised Him from the dead. He is Almighty God. He is in you. God is one. The Word was the Spirit, performing all the miraculous acts in the Old Testament. Jesus is the Spirit, performing miracles in the New Testament. The Word became Jesus. Jesus said heal the sick, cleanse the lepers, raise the dead, cast out demons. Freely you have received, freely give. Ask and you shall receive. Miracles are a way of life in the church. Don't argue doctrine but walk in the power of the Spirit of Jesus. If you can believe, all things are possible to him who believes.

The kingdom of God is a government. The governmental offices of apostles and prophets are not recognized in the cessation doctrine. No wonder they never see miracles. There have always been apostles and prophets since Jesus rose from the dead. In the last fifty years, apostles and prophets have been accepted by the church on a much wider scale. And miracles have increased dramatically. Paul laid out the church government in Corinthians.

> **Now you are the body of Christ, and members individually. And God has appointed these in the church: first apostles, second prophets, third teachers, after that miracles. (1 Corinthians 12:27–28)**

Apostles are leaders and trailblazers. Prophets hear and decree the way of the Lord, consistent with Scriptures. Teachers then teach according to proper alignment with the church government. The church of Jesus Christ is about kingdom and dominion and power to rule in the midst of your enemies.

> **Examine yourselves as to whether you are in the faith. Test yourselves. Do you not know yourselves, that Jesus Christ is in you?—unless indeed you are disqualified. (2 Corinthians 13:5)**

The very person, Jesus Christ, is in you. His glorified body is on the throne, and you are seated there with Him on the throne in the Spirit. But the Spirit of Jesus Christ is in your mortal body, able to do exceedingly abundantly above all we could ask or even think. Father, let me hear your voice today. Praise the mighty name of Jesus.

You should identify as a citizen of the kingdom of God on earth. No matter what country or nation you live in, you are in the government of God. God is now our source through faith in Him. No matter how the natural economy is performing where you live, you are operating under the covenant of wealth because of your faith in Jesus Christ. God's economy will never have a downturn. Isaac sowed in the land in famine and reaped a hundredfold in the same year. Whatever you do, do it with all of your heart as to the Lord and not to men, knowing you will receive the reward of your inheritance, for you serve the Lord Christ. If you work for the Lord, your earthly boss will always be more than satisfied. God said, "I will give you your inheritance, which is more than enough for every situation."

Decrees

- I am a king in the kingdom of God.
- The kingdom of God is expanding on the earth and in my life.

- The increase of Jesus' government and peace will have no end.
- The light will shine brighter and brighter unto that perfect day.
- I have been hidden, concealed with Christ in God.
- As He is, so am I in this world.

CHAPTER 6

Dominion Mindset

I was in the management of people for forty-two years. For seven years, I was in a factory that had a union. I watched when people came out of the union or bargaining unit and accepted a supervisory position. Many times, it was difficult for those people because they were once receiving directions, and now, they were the ones giving directions. Some of the people who were still in the union would say to the new supervisor, "Who do you think you are? Now you're the big man." For some, it was a very difficult transition, and some simply could not make the shift. They would rather refuse the promotion of pay and status than to be unpopular to their peers.

I think, in many ways, the church has suffered from the same mindset. One of the things the church has done is to try to fit in to what we were promoted out of. We were promoted out of slavery to the devil into rulership of the earth in the kingdom of God. But we would rather blend in than stand in our God-given authority in Jesus. If we don't rule the earth, then the ousted one will fill the vacuum by default. Weak managers make for weak departments, which make for weak unprofitable companies.

My people are destroyed for lack of knowledge. (Hosea 4:6)

We are not destroyed by the devil. We are destroyed because we refuse to accept and believe the promotion at the new birth that took us out of a position of slavery back into the position of managers of the earth. Strong leaders will always produce strong profits. In this is my Father glorified that you bear much fruit. I pray we no longer try to negotiate with a disgruntled devil that only wants to steal, kill, and destroy the people on the earth. He (devil) has been terminated. Man has the God-given authority to rule the earth. Let us be about our Father's business.

He who says to the wicked, "You are righteous," Him the people will curse; Nations will abhor him. But those who rebuke the wicked will have delight, and

**a good blessing will come upon them.
(Proverbs 24:24–25)**

The Biden administration is by far the most outwardly antichrist administration in my lifetime. We cannot serve two masters. I decree the light of God over all the darkness that they are promoting in our government and public schools. This is a spirit situation. When the blind leads the blind, they will both fall into the ditch. I pray the vengeance of the Lord on those keeping people in bondage. Every person's promotion to prosperous living has already been paid for by the blood of Jesus.

I decree the church of Jesus Christ accepts the mindset of a King on the earth. I decree a mindset of dominion on the sons of God. I speak to those in darkness, the devil can hold you no longer. Come out and live and prosper and laugh in the name of Jesus. Anything that has two heads is a freak. Work as unto the Lord. In whatever you do, work as unto the Lord, and He will reward you from heaven. Heaven is the richest place in the universe. The kingdom of God is in you.

Accept your promotion. Some people may never understand why you came out of darkness. I did drugs for five years. When I got saved and quit doing drugs, I lost every friend I had. They did not want to be around me because I quit getting high. I understood how they felt about me, but I knew, for me, it was a promotion. I could not serve the idol of drug use, which is a spirit of witchcraft, and Jesus Christ at the same time. I was tired of being a slave. Drugs seemed fun and were a temporary relief for me. After five years of daily use, it was no longer fun, and the devil was tightening a noose around my neck. I can remember thinking that I wished it wasn't this way, but there is no way out. God will lead you out of darkness if you are willing to be led. I have not done any drugs since 1979. You can only start from where you are. God loves you, and God will promote you. I pray you will be teachable in Jesus' name. Those who follow the Spirit of God are the sons of God. My people perish for lack of knowledge. Your days of perishing are over. You are who I say you are. I created the universe. I spoke all things into existence. You are a new creation. The old person you used to be no longer exists. "Nothing is impossible to you now because nothing is impossible to Me, and I live in you." Do not doubt it. Only believe it. It is Jesus Christ in you, the hope of glory. Rise, church of Jesus Christ, and take your rightful position in the earth realm. There is a one-world government now on earth, and it is the kingdom of God in Jesus Christ.

Be willing to believe who God says you now are. God has decreed that once you believe and confess Jesus as Lord, you become a totally new person. The old has passed away, and the new has come—the new you, the one that will rule and reign forever.

> **But what does it say? "The word is near you, in your mouth and in your heart" (that is, the word of faith which we preach): that if you confess with your mouth the Lord Jesus and believe in your heart that God raised Him from the dead, you will be saved. For with the heart on believes unto righteousness, and with the mouth confession is made unto salvation. For the Scripture says, "Whoever believes on Him will not be put to shame." (Romans 10:8–11)**

Those who know their God shall do exploits. I pray you know God has promoted you into leadership. You are appointed to rule. Stand, having done all to stand. Leadership is not always easy, but that is your job. Dominion on earth is your job. You are a king in the kingdom of God. The days of the devil telling you what to do are over. If then you have been raised with Christ, seek those things that are above, where Christ is seated at the right hand of the Father. It is now my job to enforce the Spirit of God in my environment. All lawlessness is terminated in my life in the name of Jesus.

Decrees

- I accept my position as a son of God on earth.
- This one thing I do is I forget those things that are behind.
- I go from faith to faith and from glory to glory.
- Jesus Christ is in me.
- I have a dominion mindset.
- I wish above all things that you would prosper and be in health.
- I call souls out of darkness and into your light in Jesus' name.

CHAPTER 7

The Forgiveness of Sin

If we are weak in our faith in the grace of Jesus Christ, then we will always be weak. We, as believers in Messiah, cannot move into the "new creation and kingdom of God" mindset except through grace. Grace means favor. Grace means a free gift. A better meaning is the free gift of supernatural empowerment. Jesus Christ paid the price in full for the forgiveness of sins. As far as the Father is concerned, you have never sinned a day in your life. Our part is to believe it. When we realize all our sins are forgiven, it cleanses our conscience, so we can move from condemnation and guilt into freedom and innocence for pursuit of our God-given destinies. Now you have a new employer, so to speak, with limitless benefits and opportunities. You are no longer working for a company that just wants to use you and abuse you. Now you have come to a company named Zion, whose CEO wants you to reach your highest potential and prosper beyond your wildest imagination.

God is good, and His love endures forever. Never deny what God died to gift to you. Receive it in Jesus' name.

> **Having predestined us to adoption as sons by Jesus Christ to Himself, according to the good pleasure of His will, to the praise of the glory of His grace, by which He made us accepted in the Beloved. In Him we have redemption through His blood, the forgiveness of sins, according to the riches of His grace which He made to abound toward us in all wisdom and prudence, having made known to us the mystery of his will, according to His good pleasure which He purposed in Himself, that in the dispensation of the fullness of the times He might gather together in one all things in Christ, both which are in heaven and which are on earth—in Him. (Ephesians 1:5–10)**

The mystery of His will is that God Himself, in the body of Jesus, would die for the sins of the whole world that whoever believes in Him will not perish but will rule and reign forever as heaven and earth become fully one. Always be mindful that the Father has accepted you in the Beloved. You are loved perfectly by Father's glory.

> **He has delivered us from the power of darkness and conveyed us into the kingdom of the Son of His love, in whom we have redemption through His blood, the forgiveness of sins. He is the image of the invisible God, the firstborn over all creation. (Colossians 1:13–15)**

We have the forgiveness of sins by faith in the death and resurrection of Jesus Christ. It is the righteousness of God. The Father has accepted us only by our faith in the beloved Son of God. As long as faith in Jesus Christ is active, we are grafted into the tree of life. We do not want to sin, but if we do sin, we have an advocate with God, Jesus Christ, the righteous one. God has removed us from darkness and the evil one by faith in the firstborn of the dead. Hallelujah!

The only way to manifest as a son of God is to know that Jesus has fulfilled the law. The law made sin exceedingly sinful. But the promise of Abraham was fulfilled by the sacrifice of the seed. Unless a seed falls into the earth and dies, it remains alone. For as Jonah was three days and three nights in the belly of the great fish, so will the Son of Man be three days and three nights in the heart of the earth. Jesus died for the sins of the whole world. His soul was made a sin offering. His body was dead and in the tomb, but His soul was poured out as a sin offering. But His body did not see decay, and His soul did not remain in hell. Hallelujah, it is finished! The sins of all who believe that Jesus is the Son of God and God raised Him from the dead will be forgiven. Blessed is the man to whom God imputes righteousness totally separate from the law. God imputes it to those who believe Jesus is Messiah.

Grace for eternal life is by faith on our part. The work of destroying the powers of the devil and the powers of darkness is 100 percent God's job. We receive it by believing God's report. There is a reward that every Christian will receive from the Lord, depending on what he has done for the kingdom of God after his salvation. Jesus is coming, and He will bring his reward with Him.

And he said to him, "Well done, good servant; because you were faithful in a very little, have authority over ten cities." (Luke 19:17)

Heaven and earth will be one. Those ten cities are on the earth.

The reward is 100 percent our part on what we have done with the Spirit of Jesus Christ in our earthly body after salvation.

> **For we must all appear before the judgement seat of Christ, that each one may receive the things done in the body, according to what he has done, whether good or bad. (2 Corinthians 5:10)**

The judgment seat in *Strong's Greek* is 968, and it means a rostrum. A rostrum is a raised platform on which a person stands to receive a reward. We will be rewarded at the judgment seat because Jesus has qualified us for the team. We will be rewarded for fruit bearing and harvest even to the point of giving a cold drink of water to someone in His name.

God does not want us to sin. I pray we do not want to go back into darkness and death. We can, if we choose, go back to fear or addiction or fornication. But God has put the power of His Spirit in us to choose right. It is always our choice. I pray we have no appetite for dead, rotten things anymore. Let the thief steal no more. I pray we go from success to success, from faith to faith, and from glory to glory.

Paul talked about a believer in Corinth that was in the church, but he was having sex with his mother-in-law.

It is actually reported that there is sexual immorality among you, and such sexual immorality as is not even named among the Gentiles—that a man has his father's wife! And you are puffed up, and have not rather mourned, that he who has done this deed might be taken away from among you. For I indeed, as absent in body but present in spirit, have already judged (as though I were present) him who has done this deed. In the Name of our Lord Jesus Christ, when you are gathered together, along with my spirit, with the power of our Lord Jesus Christ, deliver such a one to Satan for the destruction of the flesh, that his spirit may be saved in the day of Jesus Christ. (1 Corinthians 5:1–5)

Where sin abounds, grace abounds much more. Was that God's will and plan for that man's life? Absolutely not. Shall we continue to sin that grace may abound? God forbid. Yet God is not a jokester. Ananias and Sapphira found that out. God is not a game player. God is good. God is Holy. God is God all the time. Paul said, "The next time you meet, I will not be there physically, but I will be there in the spirit. Turn this man over to Satan for the destroying of his body, that his spirit might be saved in the day of the Lord." That is the wonderful working power of the blood of the Lamb of God. I don't know if that man received any reward at all, but Paul said that his spirit would be saved. Paul described the sin the man was actively involved in and said, "Let the devil kill his body that his spirit might be saved." Paul must have known the man still had faith in the death and resurrection of Jesus Christ. Praise God for His unspeakable gift of eternal life by faith in Jesus Christ.

Just about a year ago, I felt the Lord leading me to speak to a man who had been mayor of our town for thirty-two years. Because of COVID, it was really hard to meet. He was very ill and was about eighty-five years old. Finally, I met with him. It was just the two of us; his son and daughter left us alone. I asked him if he had ever accepted Jesus as his Lord and Savior. He said no. He was kind of a rough guy who had always run a construction company before, during, and after he was mayor. I told him God was probably not like what he was thinking. We were not going to be floating around in heaven, playing harps. God's kingdom is a government that will rule on the earth forever. I told him that he was a good mayor, and he really was. God had gifted him with the ability to be a good mayor. God's gifts are irrevocable, but he would have to be in God's kingdom. I asked him if he loved his two daughters. He said yes, a little taken aback by the question. I told him that God loved him way more than he could ever love his daughters. That jolted him, and he said, "How do we do it?" I led him in a prayer to receive Jesus as his Lord and Savior. He then got baptized.

He died about two months after that meeting. I don't know if he ever was able to do much in terms of rewards for the kingdom. I know his sins were forgiven. I do know he is alive and rejoicing and will return with the Lord when He comes. I know, by the power of the blood of Jesus, he will live forever.

Decrees

- I thank You for the forgiveness of my sins.
- My conscience is clean. I am sinless in God's eyes.

- My sins—past, present, and future—are forgiven by Jesus' blood.
- I have been released from the snare of the devil.
- I am seated with Jesus Christ on the throne right now.
- I am accepted in the Beloved.
- I decree, souls in darkness see a great light in Jesus' name.

CHAPTER 8

The New Creation

In Galatians 6:15, The Spirit through Paul said, "For in Christ Jesus neither circumcision or uncircumcision avails anything, but a new creation." It does not matter if you are a Jew or a non-Jew, what does matter is you do believe that Jesus is Messiah and He has taken away the sin of the whole world. If you believe that, then you are no longer in the old creation, but now you are a new-creation person. You are out of darkness and into light. Now you are actually light.

World in the New Testament means orderly arrangement. For four thousand years, the order arrangement of dominion on earth was a fallen angel on top. Adam's disobedience wreaked havoc in mankind. The prince of darkness brought death, poverty, sickness, chaos, and misery into creation. Mankind sank into the realm of darkness. Two thousand years ago, the last Adam, Jesus Christ, brought a new order arrangement to the earth. The new creation is that Man is once again ruling the earth. That Man is Jesus Christ. The day He died on the cross, the sins of the whole world were forgiven. From the day of His resurrection from the dead, a new creation exists on the earth. At this time, the old creation and the new creation both exist simultaneously. If you are not saved, you are still in the realm of the dead, the old creation. Jesus said, "Let the dead bury the dead." For those who confess with your mouth, the Lord Jesus and believe in your heart that God raised Him from the dead, you are new creation. The Spirit of God in Jesus Christ has come into your mortal body.

And because you are sons, God sent forth the Spirit of His Son into your hearts, crying out, "Abba! Father!" (Galatians 4:6)

Your spirit will never die and your mortal body will be raised at the coming of Jesus Christ who already has His glorified body. The old creation still exists in the lives of people who do not believe Jesus is Messiah. The baseline is faith in Jesus Christ.

The new creation continues to expand on the earth in the spirit realm since the resurrection of Jesus. As the new creation continues to increase in human beings, it actually morphs over into the natural creation. The atmosphere of the believer begins to be blessed by God and changed. Peace and joy and righteousness in the Spirit begin to appear. The kingdom of God is the new creation. It is like a mustard seed that is smaller than all seeds but continues to grow until it is the largest plant in the garden. The new creation with Jesus Christ as King will continue to overtake the earth until the old creation is no more.

> **For we who are in this tent groan, being burdened, not because we want to be unclothed, but further clothed, that mortality may be swallowed up by life. (2 Corinthians 5:4)**

The new creation is the Spirit of Jesus Christ in our mortal body. The mortal body has not yet been redeemed (glorified). It is a tent. It is a temporary house. The reason we are burdened is because we keep getting older, and people we love continue to die because our bodies are still old creation. We don't want to be unsaved (unclothed) but further clothed that the mortal body might be glorified or swallowed up by life. Praise God. The new creation by the Spirit of Jesus is devouring the old creation. The current of supernatural air of Jesus is drinking down and devouring the old creation. Where there was once darkness, only light and life will remain. Glory to God in the face of Jesus Christ.

As the revelation of God in the saints accelerates, true knowledge of Jesus in us causes darkness to be swallowed up by light. The Word says that we were once darkness, but now we are light. Messiah in you, the expectation of glory.

It seems there are many Christians who are very concerned about the end of the world. But the end of the evil one's arrangement is a very positive thing and will consummate with the Day of the Lord and the removal of darkness from our midst. *New* in Greek means "fresh." We have the fresh Spirit of God. We look for a fresh heaven and a fresh earth wherein dwells righteousness.

> **Therefore, if anyone is in Christ (Messiah), he is a new creation; old things have passed away; behold, all things have become new. Now all things are of God, Who has reconciled us to Himself through Jesus Christ, and has given us the ministry of reconciliation, that is, that God was in Christ reconciling the world (order arrangement) to Himself, not imputing their trespasses to them,**

and has committed to us the word of reconciliation. (2 Corinthians 5:17–19)

God has placed His Son, a Man, back on top of the new-world order. It is already here and has been expanding for two thousand years. God became a Man and canceled the sin debt by the shedding of His blood. If you believe and confess Jesus rose from the dead, you are new creation. God is in you now. You are over the angels now. You are seated with Jesus on the throne of God now. The angels must serve you and your words now. You have the authority of God now on earth over every fallen angel. When you are in faith, they must obey you because God dwells in you. All the promises of God are yes and amen. He said He would supernaturally bless everything we put our hand to.

In July 2022, there was a man at our church that had to have bypass surgery on his heart. He made it through surgery, but afterward, he had to be placed on a ventilator. The surgery was on a Sunday. On Monday morning, his daughter called me and said her dad was still on the vent. But he had asked for something to write on, and he wrote he wanted me to come and pray for him. It was about a forty-mile drive to the hospital. When I got there, she said that he had written "demons" on the tablet after we had talked. When I got to his room, I asked his daughter how long it would be before the nurse left so we could pray. She said, since he was on the vent and in critical condition, she was there constantly. I said, "Then let's go ahead and pray. Let's lift our hands to God. Father, in the name of Jesus, we pray for Bob's healing. Angels of the Most High God, converge upon Bob and destroy any fallen angels trying to influence his life in any way. We decree he shall live and not die and declare the works of the Lord in the name of Jesus."

The next morning, the daughter called me and asked if I had heard anything about her dad. I said I had not. She said he was off the vent, and he was telling everyone in the room that after I prayed, there was a huge angel that entered the room. All the dark angels fled when he came and the angel sat in the chair next to the bed until the ventilator was taken off him. This man had just been saved a little over a year. He was at church within a month of his surgery and is still serving God.

Bless the Lord, you His angels, who excel in strength, who do His word, heeding the voice of His word. (Psalm 103:20)

The Word of God, Jesus Christ, is in you. The angels must obey. The angels of light want to serve you, and the angels of darkness must obey you. I pray you see yourself as a new-creation conqueror from this day forward in the name of Jesus. Open your mouth wide, and I will fill it.

Decrees

- I have been made one with God in Jesus.
- Old things have passed away. I am free in Jesus' name.
- I have been anointed to rule on the earth.
- The old creation is dissolving in the heat of Holy Ghost.
- Death is swallowed up in victory.
- I am a new creation person in Jesus.
- I decree the light of God over strongholds, holding souls captive in Jesus' name.

CHAPTER 9

The Temple

The Lord instructed Moses to construct the tabernacle in intricate detail. Every material and size were specified, and the children of Israel did all the work. The measurements for where everything was to be placed in the tent were exact. God showed Moses to make a copy of the true temple in heaven, made without hands. The tabernacle was the meeting place between God and man on the earth. The tabernacle was a movable, elaborate worship tent designed by God while Israel was in the desert.

> **And he raised up the court all around the tabernacle and the altar, and hung up the screen of the court gate. So Moses finished the work. Then the cloud covered the tabernacle of meeting, and the glory of the Lord filled the tabernacle. And Moses was not able to enter the taberna-**

cle of meeting, because the cloud rested above it, and the glory of the Lord filled the tabernacle. Whenever the cloud was taken up from above the tabernacle, the children of Israel would go onward in all their journeys. But if the cloud was not taken up, then they did not journey till the day it was taken up. For the cloud of the Lord was above the tabernacle by day, and fire was over it by night, in the sight of all the house of Israel, throughout all their journeys. (Exodus 40:33–38)

Solomon built the first temple (not tabernacle) in Jerusalem (990 years BC). Ezra and Zerubbabel built the second (520 BC). In 0 BC, Jesus, the Word made flesh, arrived on the scene. The meeting place of God and Israel was about to take a radical change. The covenant terms God had made with Israel are changing.

The woman at the well told Jesus, "Our fathers worshipped on this mountain, and you, Jews, say that in Jerusalem (temple) is the place where one ought to worship."

Jesus said to her, "Woman, believe Me, the hour is coming when you will nei-

ther on this mountain, nor in Jerusalem, worship the Father. You worship what you do not know; we know what we worship, for salvation is of the Jews. But the hour is coming, and now is, when the true worshipers will worship the Father in spirit and truth; for the Father is seeking such to worship Him. God is Spirit, and those who worship Him must worship in spirit and truth."
(John 4:21–24)

God chose the descendants of Abraham to represent Him as a nation on the earth. God is a faith God. It is impossible to please God without faith. Abraham believed God for the impossible, and it was accounted to him as righteousness. God will always keep His promise if we are willing to believe and obey Him. Jesus is the Messiah that Israel was waiting on to arrive. Messiah came, but many Jews rejected Him as the Christ. The new covenant is a better covenant with better promises. The Jews who have rejected Jesus as Messiah have remained under the law of condemnation, guilt, and shame. There is an individual promise of supernatural strength and power to all who believe that Jesus is Messiah. Now, the nation of God is shifting from the natural bloodline of Abraham, Isaac, and Jacob to whoever believes that Jesus is the Son of God, and God has raised Him from the dead, the Jews first and then the Gentiles. All who call upon the name of the Lord will be saved.

Jesus began His ministry at thirty years of age. When Jesus was baptized by John the Baptist, a voice came from heaven, which said, "You are My beloved Son. In You I am well pleased." Jesus demonstrated by faith that He was going to be baptized into death for the sins of the whole world that whosoever believes in Him will not perish but have everlasting life. The Word was the Spirit moving in the Old Testament. Now Jesus is the Spirit moving in the New Testament. Glory to the name of Jesus. Shortly after the baptism of water and the Spirit, Jesus entered into Jerusalem and drove out of the temple those who were selling sheep and oxen and the money changers. The temple was supposed to be the meeting place of God and Israel, but money had definitely become an idol. The Jews were angry and said, "What sign will you show us to prove you are Messiah?"

Jesus answered and said to them, "Destroy this temple, and in three days I will raise it up." Then the Jews said, "It has taken forty-six years to build

this temple, and will you raise it up in three days." But He was speaking of the temple of His body. (John 2:19–21)

The meeting place of God and man would no longer be a tabernacle (tent) or a stone temple, but now it will be the resurrected body of Jesus Christ. Jesus clearly declares the new covenant temple is His resurrected body. The body of Jesus has been the temple of God for two thousand years and is still so right now. Jesus is upon the throne of Almighty God in His glorified body. His believers are still in tents, so to speak. We have been born again in the Spirit, and our spirit cannot die. But our bodies (tents) have not been redeemed. We have the Spirit of God in our midst, but our bodies age and die until Jesus comes. Our Spirits cannot die. Jesus said, "He who lives and believes in Me shall never die." To be absent from the body is to be present with the Lord. Death has been defeated in the eternal realm. Jesus has destroyed death and him who had the power of death that is the devil. The devil only has lies against the truth. But a lie can kill you if you believe it. We are the light of the world. We are a city set on a hill. The light destroys the darkness immediately every time. Jesus Christ is the temple of God in the new covenant. The Scripture says to believers, "Do you not now that your bodies are the temple of the Holy Ghost?" You are the body of Jesus on earth. He is on the throne of God right now in His glorified body, and you are seated with Him right now in your spirit man. The Spirit of Jesus Christ is in your mortal body right now. You are one with God. You are a son of God, born of the seed of Jesus Christ. Unless a seed falls to the ground and dies, it cannot bear fruit. Jesus was in the heart of the earth for three days and three nights. His soul was made a sin offering. But He rose from the dead. He is the firstborn of the dead. His Spirit came back into His body, and He now sits on the throne of God. Hallelujah! The Spirit of God is in you. All the power of God is in you now and is activated by faith and the name of Jesus. Greater is He that is in you than he that is in the world.

The temple Jesus entered into and drove out the money changers that took forty-six years to build was totally destroyed in AD 70 by the Romans. Jesus Christ is the new temple. It is not in the natural city of Jerusalem. Christians should not be waiting for the building of the temple in Jerusalem. Believers in Jesus Christ's resurrection from the dead are the new Jerusalem. We are the temple of God in Jesus.

For through Him we both (Jews and Gentiles) have access by one Spirit to the

Father. Now, therefore, you are no longer strangers and foreigners, but fellow citizens with the saints and members of the household of God, having been built on the foundation of the apostles and prophets, Jesus Christ Himself being the chief cornerstone, in whom the whole building, being fitted together, grows into a holy temple in the Lord, in whom you also are being built together for a dwelling place of God in the Spirit. (Ephesians 2:18–22)

Jesus Christ is now the temple of God. As believers, you are being built together as the dwelling place of the Spirit of God on the earth as the body of Jesus. We are living stones.

Coming to Him as to a living stone, rejected indeed by men, but chosen by God and precious, you also, as living stones, are being built up a spiritual house, a holy priesthood, to offer up spiritual sacrifices acceptable to God through Jesus Christ. (1 Peter 2:4–6)

Jesus' body is the new covenant temple. The church is His body on earth. Now you are the body of Christ and members individually. I pray that as individual members, we have faith to believe the investment of God has made in us to demonstrate His resurrection power in our lives. The power to rule and reign on the earth has come in the Spirit of Jesus Christ. Open your mouth wide, and I will fill it. As I told Joshua, I tell you, "No man shall be able to stand before you all the days of your life; as I was with Moses, so I will be with you. I will not leave you nor forsake you" (Joshua 1:5).

Decrees

- I offer my body as a living sacrifice for the glory of God.
- My body is the temple of God.
- Father, reveal Your Son in me.
- I am born of the Spirit of God by the Seed, Jesus Christ.
- I am a dwelling place of God on the earth.

CHAPTER 10

Dominion Restored

Dominion has been restored to Man. The power to rule the earth was given back to Man when Jesus died on the tree. The sins of all mankind were forgiven when Jesus was sacrificed as the Lamb of God that takes away the sin of the world. Whoever believes in Him shall not perish but have everlasting life. The Scripture says, "For this purpose, the Son of God was manifested that He might destroy the works of the devil." The power of the fallen angel has been destroyed by the death and resurrection of Jesus Christ. If you have received Jesus as Lord and Savior, you have been elevated to God status. You are a son of God. The son of a dog is a dog. The son of a cat is a cat. The son of a man is a man. The son of God is a God. We are one in Jesus. You have been removed from darkness.

**There is one body and one Spirit, just
as you were called in one hope of your**

calling; one Lord, one faith, one baptism; one God and Father of all, who is above all, and through all, and in you all. (Ephesians 4:4–6)

You are one body and Spirit with Jesus. God is now your Father forever. You are the fullness of the Godhead in your body. The devil can lie, but he can never change the reality that you belong to God, and God is in you. You will never be out of the presence of God one second throughout all eternity. You will never ever be alone. Glory!

There is much talk about cancel culture. I saw commercials on TV during the NCAA basketball tournament that said, "You can change history." Well, you cannot change history. The devil is a liar and murderer from the beginning. The biggest lie and the biggest cancel culture is to suppress the truth that Jesus has given supernatural power to those who believe in Him. I pray you know this. The Bible says, "My people perish for lack of knowledge." You will not perish. The people who know their God shall be strong and carry out great exploits. The body of Jesus on the earth (the church) is understanding their true status as never before. That is why, the enemy is desperate to control all media. Faith comes by hearing and hearing by the Word of God. If people hear the opportunity of living in a dimension of health, wealth, peace, and power of God, they will seize it immediately. Jesus is speaking through His Spirit to people to come out of bondage from the evil one. The devil has been defeated, and he can suppress you no more in Jesus' name.

> **For the wrath of God is revealed from heaven against all ungodliness and unrighteousness of men, who suppress the truth in unrighteousness. (Romans 1:18)**

This Scripture was given two thousand years ago. The wrath of God has been revealed from heaven that whole time. As the church of Jesus is understanding their status and resurrection power, the ability to suppress the truth of the resurrection of Jesus is becoming impossible. Jesus said, "I am the light of the world." The light is expanding in intensity and numerically, and the darkness is being destroyed.

Ever since the resurrection of Jesus from the dead, there has always been a group of men that work with the devil to suppress the truth. They know each other, and it is a concerted effort to suppress the truth of Jesus' victory. Some people do the suppressing in ignorance. But there is a group of ungodly and unrighteous men who knowingly suppress the truth of Jesus' victory for mankind. The lies and evil ways they have used to suppress and pervert the truth are being dissolved by the revealing of the Spirit of Jesus in His people on earth. God's will is for the church to rule and reign on the earth.

> **By that will we have been sanctified through the offering of the body of Jesus Christ once for all. And every priest stands ministering daily and offering repeatedly the same sacrifices (not since AD 70), which can never take away sins. But this Man, after He had offered one sacrifice for sins forever, sat down at the right hand of God, from that time waiting till His enemies are made His footstool. For by one offering He has perfected forever those who are being sanctified. (Hebrews 10:10–14)**

It takes faith to please God. Who has believed our report? And to whom has the arm of the Lord been revealed? It takes faith to believe you are no longer a son of man. But now, by faith in Jesus, you are a son of God. It takes faith to operate on the God level. You are sinless and pure in God's eyes because of your faith in the blood of Jesus. You have the Spirit of Jesus in you right now. Renew my mind until I know God loves me, and God is for me. No weapon formed against me shall prosper. I condemn every tongue that rises against me. Are you in the faith? Test yourself. Do you not know yourself that Jesus Christ is in you, not the Father, not the Holy Spirit? But you must know, Jesus Christ is in you. The Father is in you as well, but the Spirit is now the Man who defeated the devil and gave dominion of the earth back to Man.

> **That they all may be one, as You, Father,
> are in Me, and I in You; that they also
> may be one in Us, that the world may
> believe that You sent Me. And the glory
> which You gave Me I have given them,
> that they may be one just as We are one.
> (John 17:21–22)**

The devil is not a creator, he is an imitator. When Jesus says to the church, "You are one with Me, and I am one with the Father that you may be one with Us," the enemy sees the body of Jesus forming on the earth. He is imitating that with his deception of transgenders. Since a Christian is no longer a son of man but now a son of God by faith in Jesus, the enemy is telling a boy, "You can be a girl." And he is telling a girl, "You can be a cat." But God is true, and He has truly changed those who believe in Him. Offer your body as a living sacrifice, holy, acceptable to God, which is your reasonable service. Dominion has been restored to man, but God had to become Man to do it. The liberation of the earth is happening. True godly authority is being administered through the born-again sons of God on earth. The one body of Jesus on earth is rising in power (miraculous power). We love people, but through the Spirit of Jesus, we are destroying the fallen angels and their influence on people.

The Lord gives voice before His army, for His camp is very great; for strong is the One who executes His word. For the day of the Lord is very great and very terrible; who can endure it? (Joel 2:11)

The voice of the Lord is beginning to generate through His people on earth. The same voice (Word) that created all things in heaven and earth is now speaking through His people on earth. Church of Jesus Christ arise and shine, for your hour has come. The reason that the darkness and the perversion of man seems so graphic is because the light is getting brighter. Your kingdom come, Your will be done on earth as it is in heaven. The kingdom has come and is in the church.

The Lord is manifesting on His people, and the enemy knows his deceptions are being laid bare. The Lord will arise over you, and His glory will be seen upon you. The presence of God cannot be hidden. It is very apparent that the Spirit of Jesus Christ is flowing from the hearts of His chosen, destroying the lying works of the devil. Glory to the name of Jesus.

Decrees

- It is getting brighter and brighter unto that perfect day.
- The light shines, and darkness is destroyed.
- Rise, church of Jesus Christ in America.
- Rise, church of Jesus Christ in China.
- I decree the full measure of the wrath of God on the men, suppressing the truth in the name of Jesus.
- I decree light on blinded minds in Jesus' name.
- Rise, church of Jesus Christ in all nations on the earth.
- The increase of the government of God has no end.

CHAPTER 11

The Revealing of the Sons of God

The lies of the enemy that have held multitudes in bondage are being demolished by the church of Jesus Christ on earth. The nations that have been held in ignorance as to the supernatural power of the Spirit of Jesus to liberate them is being destroyed. When I say *nations*, I am referring to the people. The antichrist spirit is working to shield people from the raw power of the resurrection power of Jesus that crushes every spirit of the devil. The public-school systems in this nation have been exposed since the coronavirus. When e-learning happened, parents were able to see that the public schools were teaching their children things totally contrary to the Scriptures. When parents began to protest at the school board meetings, they were labeled domestic terrorist by the FBI. In the state of California, it is law that a baby can be killed up until twenty-eight days old with parental consent. This is the spirit of antichrist, and this is spiritual warfare. What is happening in our nation and around the world is a systematic enforcement of very grievous lies of the devil against mankind. This is a spirit issue and not a political issue. The White House nor congress nor the senate can destroy the powers of darkness operating on the earth. Woe to the politicians that have sided with the evil one. I decree the light of God exposes them. The correction will be in the spirit realm, not in the natural realm. The Spirit of God operating through the church will be the solution. The church is the only entity on earth that has the power to destroy the lying wonders we are witnessing.

I had a store manager for about twenty-five years, and she was a good worker and a good person. Many times, I would speak to her about addressing employees that were not performing the way they could, and she would always say, "I would rather just show them by my example of hard work." She was a good worker, and she never missed work. And she was honest. But there is a time when, if you are the one in charge, you must pointedly address the unacceptable behavior of what you have been given to supervise. The church has dominion over the earth. We must open our mouths and decree the law of the Lord Jesus. We are powerful, not powerless, unless we remain silent. Open your mouth wide, and I will fill it.

Let no one deceive you with empty words, for because of these things the wrath of God comes upon the sons of disobedience. Therefore do not be partakers with them. For you were once darkness, but now you are light in the Lord. Walk as children of light (for the fruit of the Spirit (Light) is in all goodness, righteousness, and truth), finding out what is acceptable to the Lord. And have no fellowship with the unfruitful works of darkness but rather expose them. (Ephesians 5:6–11)

Jesus has given us rule of the earth. It is our job. Yes, we do lead by example, but we also expose. We call out the unacceptable behavior of our subordinates. We are now light in the Lord. We are in Jesus, and Jesus is in us. He is the light of the world, and we are now the light of the world. We speak to the darkness, and the darkness cannot remain in the name of Jesus. As ambassadors of the kingdom of God, when we speak, He backs us up. We are only enforcing His rules of conduct. God threw Satan out of heaven in a second. Jesus said, "I saw him fall like lightning." That is swift justice. When you understand your position and your authority in Jesus, He will remove any demon from your atmosphere with the same swiftness. Praise God.

Do you have the faith to believe that your superior in this kingdom business will back you up when you confront that which you know is a cancer working in your jurisdiction?

Then He spoke a parable to them, that men always ought to pray and not lose heart, saying: "There was in a certain city a judge who did not fear God nor regard man. "Now there was a widow in that city; and she came to him, saying, 'Get justice for me from my adversary.' And he would not for a while; but afterward he said within himself, 'Though I do not fear God nor regard man, yet because this widow troubles me I will avenge her, lest by her continual coming she weary me.'" Then the Lord said, "Hear what the unjust judge said. And shall God not avenge His own elect who cry out day and night to Him, though He bears long with them?

I tell you He shall avenge them speedily. Nevertheless, when the Son of Man comes, will He really find faith on the earth?" (Luke 18:1–8)

"I am your superior. You are My focal point. I am asking you to cry out to Me. I want you to express your dissatisfaction with your adversary. People are not your problem. Your adversary is the problem. I tell you, I am the righteous judge. I want you to cry out in faith that I will answer you quickly."

Do I not hate them, O Lord, who hate You? I hate them with perfect hatred; I count them my enemies. (Psalm 139:21–22)

Cry out against the abortion spirit. Cry out against the antichrist systems in your government and public schools. Cry out against the child sex trade and the traders themselves. Cry out against the poverty spirit. Cry out against the witchcraft spirit of drugs and pharma. Cry out against the money cartels, financing the antichrist activities.

Church of Jesus Christ believe and take God at His Word. The Scriptures cannot be broken. The laws are forever settled in heaven. Faith from Christians will bring swift justice from Almighty God. Demonic strongholds are destroyed by our faith-filled words.

It is our job to expose and reprove the lawlessness. Decree the prophetic decrees of the Scriptures, and the very Word settled in heaven will answer with righteous fire.

God is for us, and God is in us in the Spirit of Jesus. Nothing can separate us from the love of God in Jesus Christ our Lord. As the Father reveals His Son in us, we understand our true calling as heirs of God.

For I consider that the sufferings of this present time are not worthy to be compared with the glory which shall be revealed in us. For the earnest expectation of the creation waits for the revealing of the sons of God. For the creation was subjected to futility, not willingly, but because of Him who subjected it in hope; because the creation itself also will be delivered from the bondage of corruption into the glorious liberty of the children of God. For we know that the whole creation groans and labors with birth pangs together until now. Not only that, but we also who have the

firstfruits of the Spirit, even we ourselves groan within ourselves, eagerly waiting for the adoption, the redemption of the body. (Romans 8:18–23)

When Adam fell, every created thing under his dominion fell into the bondage of decay and death. As the revelation of the Son becomes greater in His people, the darkness has to give way. The fear of the Lord is to hate evil. The church is stepping into the fullness of the stature of Jesus. God is calling on the church to call out for His vengeance, believing it will be swift. All of creation, including the animals, the birds, the fish, the trees, and the ground itself, is crying out, "Come on, church, you are filled with Jesus. Acknowledge the evil, and cry out for vengeance from the righteous Father."

Decrees

- I shall live and not die and declare the works of the Lord.
- Whatever the Father says is what I do.
- Father, let me hear Your voice today.
- The righteous shall inherit the land and dwell in it forever.

- I decree the light of God over the antichrist spirit in Jesus' name.
- I decree the zeal of the Father's house overtake you this day.

CHAPTER 12

The Day of the Lord

The Day of the Lord is a time every Christian should look forward to with great anticipation. The victory of Jesus over the fallen angels that was accomplished at His death and resurrection in the eternal realm will be executed in the temporary realm. The devil knows that Man has taken back dominion of the earth from angels. When the church believes Man has taken back dominion of the earth, mortality will be swallowed up by life. Many Christians have a mentality like the ten spies who could only see the giants and not the promises. The earth is the Lord's and the fullness thereof. God speaks to us and says, "I have given you the land. Now go and possess it." Everything that can be shaken will be shaken and removed so that the things that cannot be shaken may remain. The kingdom of God cannot be shaken and will remain. The kingdom of God is in you.

The heaven, even the heavens, are the Lord's; but the earth He has given to the children of men. (Psalm 115:16)

The fallen angels are still affecting man and the earth in the temporary realm through people that are being controlled by the fallen angels. The devil orchestrates his plans to steal, kill, and destroy through mankind. The born-from-above people of God are used to give life and life more abundantly. As God continues to reveal to man that all the power of the enemy is destroyed by faith in Jesus, the Spirit of Jesus in them is destroying the temporary darkness (sickness, poverty, fear, hopelessness). The mass shootings we see so often are people operating under the lying power of the fallen angels. Many people blame God for tragedies, but it is the work of the evil one.

For it is the God who commanded light to shine out of darkness, who has shone in our hearts to give the light of the knowledge of the glory of God in the face of Jesus Christ. (2 Corinthians 4:6)

The shooting in the Christian school in Nashville, Tennessee, I believe, was a result of the influence of a fallen angel in that person's life. I think, when you do not know how much the Father loves you, it leaves you vulnerable to the enemy's influence. If he can get you concentrating on the wrongs that you believe have been done to you, then you begin to think somebody has to pay for this. Failure to forgive will prevent God from performing restoration in your life.

Last Sunday night, I received a text from a girl that had worked for me for about twenty years in the marketplace. She wanted to know if I was still up. I called her. She said her son, who has autism, had a seizure. He is sixteen years old. They were in ER when I called. She said, on the way to the hospital, she didn't know if he was going to live, and she asked him what he was feeling. He said that he felt like he was trapped behind a door, and there were black creatures trying to get him to do something very terrible with his body. He said his aunt, grandma, and grandpa were there, telling him that he had to fight. All three of them then told him to call Dwight. That is when his mom texted me. His aunt, grandma, and grandpa were all Christians, and I had preached their funerals. I asked his mom if I could speak with him. She handed him the phone. They were still in the emergency room. We confirmed his faith in Jesus as Lord and Savior. After that, I commanded every fallen angel influencing him to be destroyed in the name of Jesus. I then asked him how he felt, and he said they were gone. I called his mom fifteen minutes later, and she said he was fine now. He was at church on Sunday and praising the Lord Jesus.

The Day of the Lord will be a day (time) when the violent passion (wrath) of the Lord will come upon the world—the world, meaning the temporary arrangement of the fallen angels controlling things on earth. The wrath will come upon all those who willingly suppress the truth of the new-creation life in God in Jesus. Those who loved darkness instead of light will suffer the destruction of the kingdom of darkness.

For God did not appoint us to wrath, but to obtain salvation through our Lord Jesus Christ. (1 Thessalonians 5:9)

We are one with Jesus and the Father. The Spirit of God has taken over our bodies. Jesus the Man, the Son of God, suffered the wrath of God for all men on the tree. The sin of every man is forgiven but especially those who believe. It was done one time for all people. God will not strike the rock again. We are rescued and safe in Jesus. No evil shall befall you.

But the day of the Lord will come as a thief in the night, in which the heavens

will pass away with a great noise, and the elements will melt with fervent heat; both the earth and the works that are in it will be burned up. Therefore, since all these things will be dissolved, what manner of persons ought you to be in holy conduct and godliness, looking for and hastening the coming of the day of the Lord, because of which the heavens will be dissolved, being on fire, and the elements will melt with fervent heat? Nevertheless we, according to His promise, look for new heavens and a new earth in which righteousness dwells. (2 Peter 3:10–13)

A few things to note in the Scriptures in the *Greek Strong's Concordance*: The words *pass away* 3928 is to be gone. The word *elements* is 4747 and means orderly arrangement. The word *dissolved* is 3089, which means to loosen or put off. The order arrangement of the evil one still existing in the temporary realm (that which can be seen with the natural eye) will be removed. Wherever the devil still inhabits will be loosened and removed from the earth and in the middle of heaven. He was cast out of the third heaven when he tried to sit in God's place. *New* means "fresh." Christians are already new-creation people with the Spirit of Jesus dwelling in them. When Jesus comes in His glorified body in flames of fire, our bodies will be glorified as well. Christ is all in all. There will be no more effects of the fall of Adam (death, sin, decay, poverty, sickness, anger, wrath, murder, and malice). God is a consuming fire, and all evil will be consumed when the last Adam returns.

> But I do not want you to be ignorant, brethren, concerning those who have fallen asleep, lest you sorrow as others who have no hope. For if we believe that Jesus died and rose again, even so God will bring with Him those who sleep in Jesus. For this we say to you by the by the word of the Lord, that we who are alive and remain until the coming of the Lord will by no means precede those who are asleep. For the Lord will descend from heaven with a shout, with the voice of an archangel, and with the trumpet of God. And the dead in Christ will rise first. Then we who are alive and remain shall be caught up together with them in the

clouds to meet the Lord in the air. And thus we shall always be with the Lord. (1 Thessalonians 4:13–18)

If you believe Jesus died and rose again, then know that God will bring with Him those who died in Jesus. He will bring with Him those who died. They are as alive as Jesus. Jesus said, "Whoever lives and believes in Me shall never die." So what died if a believer never dies? The body died. Jesus is bringing with Him all those Christians whose bodies died. To be absent from the body is to be present with the Lord. Jesus is bringing with Him the spirits of the people who died in faith. But we who are alive and remain on the Day of the Lord will not precede those who died. The believers whose bodies ceased to function and died experienced physical death. We who are alive and remain will not precede them. The dead bodies of those coming with the Lord will be made alive. The dead body was buried or cremated. The dead body was planted in the earth, so to speak. Jesus said that what you sow is not the body that shall be. I have done many funerals of Christians. The body is dead, but their spirit is with the Lord. When Jesus comes, that dead body will resurrect a glorious body—a glorious body like Jesus' glorious body. Then we who remain will be seized by life and meet the Lord in the air. It is not the sky. It is the lower air we breathe. The Spirit is the breath of God. That body will not be in the ground but in the air or breath of God. We are surrounded right now by so great a cloud of witnesses. When Jesus is revealed from heaven, that cloud of witnesses will be seen. We will meet the Lord in the cloud of witnesses, not the sky. The devil and his evil, murderous kingdom (arrangement) will be loosened and dissolved by the fire of the Spirit of God. That same cleansing fire will cause everything dead to come back to life. Heaven and earth will be one with nothing that defiles ever again. And there shall be no more curse. But the throne of God and of the Lamb shall be in it, and His servants shall serve Him. There is no night there, and they shall reign forever and ever.

We do not determine the Day of the Lord. We have an assignment from the Lord: occupy until I come. Do business until I come. You have overcome. You are not a slave. You are a king on earth, demonstrating the kingdom of God. Freely you have received, freely give. Pull people out of death, poverty, and slavery by faith in the name of Jesus. Introduce them to a lifestyle of more than enough as God as their only source.

Decrees

- It is the love of God that leads people to repentance.
- Thank God for His indescribable gift of Jesus Christ.

- The evil has had its day and is passing away.

- Father, avenge me of my adversary in Jesus' name.

- An exceeding weight of glory is being revealed in His saints.

- There is no wisdom or understanding or counsel against the Lord.

Idols

The devil's power over mankind was destroyed two thousand years ago by the death and resurrection of the Man, Jesus Christ. Even though the devil and the other fallen angels were defeated, we do not see all their activities eliminated. If he is defeated, how does he still wreak havoc in the children of men?

> **You have put all in subjection under him, He left nothing that is not put under him. But now we do not yet see all things put under him. But we see Jesus, who was made a little lower than the angels, for the suffering of death crowned with glory and honor, that He, by the grace of God, might taste death for everyone. (Hebrews 2:8–9)**

Jesus is the only Man who died and was raised from the dead and is still alive today in His body. Jesus' body is glorified. By grace, by the supernatural empowerment of God, Jesus tasted death for every man and woman who has lived or ever will live. To be delivered from death, you must believe Jesus is the Son of God and confess that with your mouth. By faith in Messiah's death and resurrection, we are born again. But we are born again in the Spirit that which is flesh is flesh and that which is spirit is spirit.

The devil is an angel with great deceptive ability. He convinced many angels to side with him in an attempt to overthrow God. He convinced Eve that God was holding out on her and that if she ate of the tree of knowledge of good and evil, it would be to her advantage. The devil always uses arguments against the truth. Jesus said to the Father, "Your word is truth." The Scriptures cannot be broken. What God says, He means if you do what God says you will prosper, if you don't do what God says you will suffer.

The enemy is forever defeated. He is going from the realm of the dead and darkness into the lake of fire.

The whole of the human race was lifted when Jesus rose from the dead. Those who believe in His resurrection and say so are transferred out of death into life and light, for those who do not believe in Jesus remain in death and darkness, even though the price has been paid for their freedom. The Spirit is a down payment in the believer until the full purchase, the redemption of the body.

The devil and his angels can only buy time to remain out of the lake of fire. He does this by using idols. An idol is anything that is regarded higher than God in anyone's life.

I Am the Lord your God, who brought you out of the land Egypt, out of the house of bondage. You shall have no other gods before me. (Exodus 20:2–3)

The first commandment in the old covenant is to not have anything of more value in your life than God. God is always first. The same is true in the new covenant. The enemy knows that, so he tries to put something, anything, above God in everyone's life. He already has sway over every unbeliever's life. They are bound in everlasting darkness. To keep a believer from fully manifesting as a son of God, the devil tries to place some person or thing above the believer's faith and loyalty to God. The body desires what is contrary to the Spirit, and the Spirit desires what is contrary to the body. It is the mind or soul of the believer that decides what the body will do. God made His decision, and Jesus died to destroy the power of the body to rule in a believer's life. Greater is He that is in you than he that is in the world. The Spirit of Jesus in you will never sin. Your mind (soul) must be transformed by the Scriptures to demolish the devil's lies. The more Scripture that you can study and get revelation on, the more you know God is good, and He wants you to live in that goodness. God's Scriptures always lead to health, wealth, joy, peace, love, faithfulness, and self-control. When your mind has been renewed by the Scriptures, then the Spirit of God flows freely through your mind and body, and your life starts looking like supernatural blessing.

I am going to list a few idols that the devil uses to hinder the church and hinder the manifestation of God's presence in the believer. The Bible still talks about warfare that the church must participate in. We love people, but we do not love the devil or the idols that he uses to weaken the church and keep unbelievers blind.

For though we walk in the flesh, we do not war according to the flesh. For the weapons of our warfare are not carnal but mighty in God for the pulling down

of strongholds, casting down arguments and every high thing that exalts itself against the knowledge of God, bringing every thought into captivity to the obedience of Christ, and being ready to punish all disobedience when your obedience is fulfilled. (2 Corinthians 10:3–6)

The devil uses education to be contrary to the Scriptures. When people believe these teachings for the truth, a stronghold is formed in their mind, and they are controlled by a lie. This is obvious in the public-school system and state universities. The enemy uses television, radio, and social media to educate people with lies contrary to God's word. That is how an idol is used. The idol is not anything but the demon behind the idol that gains control in that person's life.

Religion

It might sound strange to some, but religion is one of the most powerful idols that the enemy uses. There is a teaching in many mainline Christian denominations that says all the gifts of the Spirit, such as tongues, healings, and miracles, ceased with the twelve original apostles. This is called cessation theology. I believe it is a doctrine of the devil.

But this Man, after He had offered one sacrifice for sins forever, sat down at the right hand of God, from that time waiting till His enemies are made His footstool. (Hebrews 10:12–13)

Jesus' blood was shed to forgive our sins. After He rose from the dead, He was talking to His disciples, and He told them to wait in Jerusalem to be endued with power from on high. He said, "You are going to need My Spirit to perform miracles to make My enemies My footstool." If cessation teaching is true, Jesus will never come. Greater is He that is in you than he that is in the world. Ask Jesus to baptize you with fire and the Holy Ghost and start working the works of God. Paul said, "I pray in tongues more than you all." I wish that you all prayed in tongues. He that prays in tongues builds himself up. Do it when you are alone, and let God strengthen your inner man. Desire to prophesy. Prophecy is greater than tongues because it builds up other Christians. Allow the Spirit of Jesus to flow freely in your life for the glory of the Father. God is a miracle-working God.

Mammon

Jesus specifically mentions mammon or money as a powerful idol. He said, "You cannot serve God and wealth." You cannot serve two masters; you will be loyal to one and despise the other. Tithing is a powerful way to break the power of mammon. Many good people have gone to Washington, DC, only to be destroyed through the fallen angels working behind the idol of money. Seek first the kingdom of God and His righteousness, and all these things will be added to you. Put God first in your life, and He will be your abundant supplier. To believe and obey God's promises in the Scriptures prevents an idol from establishing a foothold in a believer's life.

Abortion

Molech is an idol of child sacrifice. This demonic teaching that is exalted above the knowledge of God in many lives has cost the lives of over sixty million babies since 1973 in this country. In California, in 2023, it is legal to kill a baby up to twenty-eight days old. I decree the light of God on the governor and legislators in that state in the name of Jesus. God is life, and He desires that none perish, but all come to repentance in Jesus' name. If you have had an abortion, ask for God's forgiveness, and let God use the rest of your life for the expansion of the kingdom of God on earth. Decree the light of God over the spirit of abortion on the earth.

Drugs

The word *witchcraft* in the Greek is *pharmakeia* (Strongs 5331). It is where we get our word *pharmacy*. The demonic teaching that you need medication for depression and fear is not from the Scriptures. You don't need pot, meth, or any spell-binding spirit as an idol. The Father and Jesus are perfect in you. Perfect love casts out all fear. Have no anxiety about anything but in everything by prayer and supplication with thanksgiving, let your request be known to God. The Father would say unto you, Jesus and I are at complete rest, and We are in you. I will teach you a peace that surpasses all understanding. Ask of Me what you need to learn. I pray the spirit of witchcraft broken in everyone reading this book in the name of Jesus. God does not need a supplement; he is the Most High God, and He is in you.

The body

The Lord wants your body to be a temple of His Spirit in the earth realm, a dwelling place for His Spirit on the earth. God has put a desire for sexual relations in most people. God has also provided a solution for this desire.

Nevertheless, because of sexual immorality, let each man have his own wife, and let each woman have her own husband. (1 Corinthians 7:2)

Any sexual gratification outside the marriage of a man and woman is idolatry. Regardless of your past, a decision to follow God's guidelines will destroy the idol's power. God has provided a way to meet every need a person has in life. God's way is the authorized and fulfilling way and gives no place to the devil.

Secret societies

There are several secret societies. The one that is prominent in our area is Freemasonry. I first was informed about the Freemasons through the teaching of Derek Prince. Many of the successful people in our area belonged to the lodge. I worked with a man I thought very highly of in about 1982, and he encouraged me to seek entry because it would help me financially. I had just gotten saved (1979) and had two small children, so I did not pursue membership.

I began to preach the gospel in 1992. I stayed in the marketplace, even though I was preaching. One night, a man came to the restaurant and wanted to speak with me. He told me that he had just come from the Freemason lodge, and he had been raised from the dead. This man had just recently began walking with the Lord. He said he was entering the third degree of the Masons. He said they placed a hood over his head, and he was led into another room. They simulated his death with a blow to the head, and he was lowered to the floor. He said he was then raised by three secret words and a secret handshake and grip. He said he had made oaths that if he told any secrets of the craft that his tongue should be pulled out by the roots and his neck cut from ear to ear. None of the three secret words he was raised with was Jesus. He left the lodge.

Jesus said, "Again you have heard that it was said of those of old, 'you shall not swear falsely, but shall perform your oaths to the Lord.' But I say to you, do not swear at all: neither by heaven, for

it is God's throne; nor by the earth, for it is His footstool; nor by Jerusalem, for it is the city of the great King. Nor shall you swear by your head, because you cannot make one hair white or black. But let your 'Yes' be 'Yes', and your 'No', 'No'. For whatever is more than these is from the evil one." (Matthew 5:33–37)

I have talked to several men, and they were all surprised by the hoodwink and the oaths and simulations in the three degree. It says in the Scriptures, "Death and life are in the power of the tongue." The manifestation of the sons of God has been greatly hindered by Christians becoming Freemasons and speaking the curses over themselves. There is nothing secret about the gospel of Jesus Christ. Jesus' name is not a secret name. He is not a generic God. On the dollar bill, it says, "In God we trust." But for a Christian, our God has a specific name, and it is neither secret nor generic. There is no other name under heaven whereby men might be saved.

I asked a man several years ago if he was a Freemason. He said he used to be, but he had gotten out. I asked him if he had ever canceled the curses he had spoken over himself. He said he had not. He renounced the curses he had spoken. He said, "I have never felt so free in my life." It is important to say off what curses were spoken over yourself. Renounce (say off) the hidden things of darkness in the name of Jesus.

Therefore whatever you have spoken in the dark will be heard in the light, and what you have spoken in the ear in inner rooms will be proclaimed on the housetops. (Luke 12:3)

There are many more idols, but the main thing is to keep Jesus first place in your life.

Decrees

- I decree every demon behind an idol is destroyed by the light of God so the people can go free in the name of Jesus.
- An idol is always a counterfeit for the real blessing God wants to give His children.
- Seek first the kingdom of God and His righteousness, and everything will be added to you in Jesus' name.

CHAPTER 14

Arise and Shine Church

Supernatural light has been flooding the earth realm since the Word became a Man to take back the authority of the earth. Jesus said, "I am the light of the world."

In Him was life, and the life was the light of men. And the light shines in darkness, and the darkness did not comprehend it. (John 1:4–5)

The darkness that the devil and the fallen angels are chained in will never overtake the light. On the contrary, the light destroys the darkness wherever it goes. Jesus said, "I have a baptism to be baptized with, and how distressed am I till it is accomplished!" He was talking about the baptism of death He was to die for the sins of all mankind at the cross. He was baptized into death. His soul was made a sin offering. He poured out His soul to death, and He was numbered with the transgressors. It was in the spirit realm that He won our victory of eternal life. To this day, there is still just one body that has risen from the dead and is glorified, never to die again. When Jesus was raised from the dead in the spirit realm, He triumphed publicly over the fallen angels. His resurrected spirit returned to His physical body, bringing it back to life forever. He ministered forty days and then returned to the Father's throne.

Jesus is the High Priest forever. With His own blood entered the most holy place in the new creation to obtain eternal redemption. After He sat down at the Father's right hand on the throne, there was an outpouring of His Spirit back into the earth realm. This was the outpouring of the power of the Spirit Jesus into His church. It takes power to demolish lying strongholds. The light of God was expanded not only to those in the upper room, but there were also three thousand souls that heard and believed that Jesus had risen from the dead. Then a few days later, the number of those who believed had increased to five thousand. The kingdom of God has been expanding on the earth since that time.

Another parable He put forth to them, saying: "The Kingdom of heaven is like a mustard seed, which a man took and sowed in his field, which indeed

**is the least of all the seeds; but when
it is grown it is greater than the herbs
and becomes a tree, so that the birds of
the air come and nest in its branches."
(Matthew 13:31–32)**

Jesus was the seed. Unless a seed falls to the ground and dies, it remains alone. Jesus was in the ground three days and then rose. Jesus is the light of the world. There was one light, then there was three thousand, then five thousand. I read today where it is estimated that there are 2.6 billion Christians on the earth. That is a lot of light. The darkness is being exposed and destroyed by the light. A man told me today, he read that there are three thousand souls being saved every hour on earth. Praise the Lord.

God can never be defeated or destroyed. God is Almighty. He is the only Creator. Jesus said, "Pray this way to the Father, 'Your kingdom come, Your will be done on earth as it is in heaven.'" Jesus said after his resurrection that all authority had been given to Him in heaven and on earth. Jesus has given that same authority to His believers. "I am the light of the world, and I am in you. Occupy until I come." The earth is the Lord's and the fullness thereof.

No matter what your eschatology is, it should be clear that man will not remain in heaven but will eventually return and rule earth forever. Jesus was a man in a body made of earth. When He died for the sins of the world, it had already been prophesied that His body would not decay or return to dust.

For David says concerning Him: "I foresaw the Lord always before my face, for He is at my right hand, that I may not be shaken. Therefore my heart rejoiced, and my tongue was glad; moreover my flesh also will rest in hope. For You will not leave my soul in Hades, nor will you allow Your Holy One to see corruption." (Acts 2:25–27)

David was not prophesying about himself. David was prophesying about Jesus. David's soul is with the Lord, but his body is still in the ground. Jesus' soul was raised from hell, and His body came alive forever. There is a Man made of the earth, sitting on the throne of God right now. Hallelujah!

Jesus will send His angels, and the tares will be removed first.

He said to them, "An enemy has done this." The servants said to him, "Do

you want us then to go and gather them up?" But he said, "No, lest while you gather up the tares you also uproot the wheat with them. Let both grow together until the harvest, and at the time of harvest I will say to the reapers, 'First gather together the tares and bind them in bundles to burn them, but gather the wheat into the barn.'"
Matthew 13:28–30

Jesus said, "First, gather the tares." He did not say, "First, gather the wheat." The devil does not own anything in heaven or earth. He is a thief. Let the thief steal no more.

Arise, shine; for your light has come! And the glory of the Lord is risen upon you. For behold, the darkness shall cover the earth, and deep darkness the people; but the Lord will arise over you, and His glory will be seen upon you. The Gentiles shall come to your light, and kings to the brightness of your rising. (Isaiah 60:1–3)

Paul said, "My little children, I labor again until Jesus Christ is formed in you." He is saying, "I want you to know who you are. I want you to know your new identity. I want you to know the Son of God is in you. Father God is in you, and We have great things for you to accomplish and enjoy. The kingdom of God is in you. Your portion is greatness on the earth."

Jesus is saying, "When I died, you died. When I rose, you rose. The day you gave your life to Me, I did a personality transplant on you. No surgeon ever does a heart transplant and leaves the old heart in the body. I removed your old personality, and I gave you Mine. The old you have been demolished and removed. The finest material in the universe has been brought in by God Himself. My Father and I have renovated and revitalized your inside. We are excited to guide you into your new hope and future. Be excited about your future, We will complete what We have started."

He answered and said to them: "He who sows the good seed is the Son of Man. The field is the world, the good seeds are the sons of the kingdom, but the tares are the sons of the wicked one. The enemy who sowed them is the devil,

"the harvest is the end of the age, and
the reapers are the angels. Therefore as
the tares are gathered and burned in
the fire, so it will be at the end of this
age. The Son of Man will send out His
angels, and they will gather out of His
kingdom all things that offend, and
those who practice lawlessness, and will
cast them into the furnace of fire. There
will be wailing and gnashing of teeth.
"Then the righteous will shine forth as
the sun in the kingdom of their Father.
He who has ears to hear, let him hear!"
(Matthew 13:37–43)

There will be a rapture out of the kingdom of God
on earth for all things that offend and those who practice
lawlessness. Father has given the nations of the earth to
Jesus as His inheritance. Wealth and riches are flowing into
the hands of the church to finance and create new media
streams. This will allow release of revelation knowledge of
Jesus through the airwaves to the multitudes. The kingdom
of God is not in word but in power.

Romans 1:18 and 2 Thessalonians 2:7 have a word
in common that is rarely connected. One reason they are

not connected is that in the KJV and the NKJV versions, the translation in English is two different words. The word in Romans 1:18 is *suppress*. The Greek in *Strong's* is 2722, which means "to hold down." The word in 2 Thessalonians 2:2 is *restrains*, but in the Greek, it is 2722 as well. In Romans 1:18, it talks about the wrath of God being revealed against men holding down the truth. In 2 Thessalonians 2:7, sometime in the last forty years, the word *he* that now restrains (suppresses) was changed to a capital H, *He*, meaning God. It is not God suppressing the truth, and it is not God who is going to be taken out of the way. As soon as all the antichrist-advocate men and fallen angels are taken out of the way by the decrees of the church, operating as sons of God on earth, then the Lord will come. Then the lawless one will be revealed, whom the Lord will consume with the breath of His mouth and the brightness of His coming. When the church has removed all the lies, satan will be cast from the earth, like lightning into the lake of fire. Praise the holy name of Jesus forever and ever, world without end. Amen.

Decrees

- It is Jesus Christ in you, the hope of glory.
- I decree you know Jesus Christ is in you.

- Don't look here or there. Behold, the kingdom of God is in you.
- I decree rivers of living waters flow from your heart and mouth, releasing words of life and deliverance into your atmosphere in Jesus' name.
- I decree the full wrath of God on the men, suppressing the truth in Jesus' name.
- I decree the light of God over every antichrist structure in the earth realm.

CHAPTER 15

The Revelation of Jesus Christ

In order to have a dominion mindset, you must truly believe you have dominion. God gave dominion of the earth to man in Genesis 1:26. Dominion of the earth was given by the man, Adam, to a fallen angel. Jesus Christ, the Son of God, took dominion of the earth back for man through His crucifixion and resurrection from the dead.

And Jesus came and spoke to them, saying, "All authority has been given to Me in heaven and earth." (Matthew 28:18)

Jesus cried out from the cross as He was dying, "It is finished." The Lamb of God had been sacrificed for the sins of the whole world. The price for the forgiveness of sins had been paid by God Himself (Word) in the form of a man. The Word was the Spirit of God in the Old Testament. Nothing was made that He did not make. Jesus

Christ is the Spirit of God in the New Testament. Jesus is now the name above all names. Rulership of the earth was forever shifted back to men who believe Jesus is the Son of God and God raised Him from the dead. Dominion of the earth will never be in question again because Jesus Christ is on the throne of God.

The book of Revelation of Jesus Christ is not the revelation of the end-times. It is revealing of Jesus Christ. The word *revelation* in the *Greek Strong's* 602 is apocalypse. Apocalypse has been defined as the end of the world in some places and movies. But the Greek defines it as to disclose or take the cover off. The book of Revelation of Jesus Christ takes the cover off all that was done in the spirit realm from His birth till when Jesus died and was dead three days and rose from the dead and started the new creation of Man. This new creation is not waiting to take authority of the earth. The new creation of Man already has all authority on earth.

> **And when He had said this, He showed them His hands and His side. Then His disciples were glad when they saw the Lord. So Jesus said to them again, "Peace to you! As the Father has sent Me, I also send you." (John 20:20–21)**

"You have My peace. You have My power. You have My victorious Spirit. You have dominion of the earth; occupy until I come. The fallen angels have been defeated if I live in you."

However, we speak wisdom among those who are mature, yet not the wisdom of this age, nor of the rulers of this age, who are coming to nothing. But we speak the wisdom of God in a mystery (hidden truth), the hidden wisdom which God ordained before the ages for our glory, which none of the rulers of this age knew; for had they known, they would not have crucified the Lord of glory. (1 Corinthians 2:6–8)

The fallen angels use men just as God uses men. Satan entered into Judas at the last supper to betray Jesus. Fallen angels entered into Herod, Pilate, and the high priest to crucify the Son of Man. But if the powers and principalities of darkness had known it was going to be their demise, they would have never done it. Hades means the realm of the dead and the realm of the unseen. The Revelation of Jesus Christ discloses what happened in the eternal spirit realm from His birth to the cross to the throne room in heaven.

Almost everyone I know was taught the book of Revelation is an account of the end-times. The books and movies like *Left Behind* and *The Late Great Planet Earth* shaped our theologies. We were taught to be ready for the rapture so we would not be left behind for the great tribulation. If Holy Spirit and all believers are raptured out of the earth, how could anyone ever get saved. You would be saved by the shedding of your own blood without the Spirit of God. That is a doctrine of the devil. If Jesus Christ is in you, and He is your righteousness, how could you be left behind? This is impossible. The rapture mentality has had a tremendously negative effect on the church. I have preached funerals for good Christian men who believed they would be raptured and had no life insurance for the wives. Others believed they would be raptured and never really accomplished what God had for them because "what would it matter anyway? We are not going to be here." One of the reasons the media is controlled by men serving the antichrist spirit is because the church has not tapped into the supernatural wealth of dominion. The rapture is an escape mentality and is not consistent with how God dealt with His people in the Scriptures. "Be strong and of good courage, for to this people, you shall divide as an inheritance, the land which I swore to their fathers to give them. I have given you the land. Now go and possess it."

The revelation of Jesus Christ was given to John. He was imprisoned on the island of Patmos because he believed Jesus was Messiah, and He had risen from the dead. John was in the Spirit on the Lord's Day. He did not see any of the uncovering of Jesus with his natural eyes.

There are two main things I want to address. The first is that this is a Spirit revealing. Eye has not seen or ear heard or has the heart imagined the things that God has prepared for those who love him. But He has revealed it to us through His Spirit. God revealed Jesus' death and resurrection to John in the Spirit, not the end-times. John had seen and talked to Jesus after His resurrection, but now he is going to be shown the extent of victory that was accomplished at the cross.

The victory of Jesus in the eternal realm is finished. The devil is defeated on earth for anyone that has received the Spirit of Jesus. Jesus disarmed principalities and powers. He made a public spectacle of them, triumphing over them in it. This public routing was in the Spirit over the fallen angels. God and all the angels saw this public defeat of the enemy. The Revelation shows Jesus defeating all the ranks of the fallen angels. Jesus, the King of the Jews, defeated the prince of darkness and all powers of darkness in the Spirit at the battle of Armageddon. The kings (fallen angels) of death, sickness, disease, poverty, fear, and lust were all destroyed in the spirit realm by Jesus. It is finished. Jesus destroyed death and him who had the power of death—that is, the devil. Then Jesus returned to His body and is now on the throne of God. There is not a future natural battle to fight for Christians to be victorious. We are victorious. We are to fight the good fight of faith. It is done. God is alive inside all His believers.

The second thing about the Revelation of Jesus Christ is that it is not in chronological order. Jesus said, "I am He who was and is and is to come." I am going to say it again, it is the uncovering of Jesus Christ as a person in the Spirit and His accomplishment of the crucifixion and resurrection.

And when I saw Him, I fell at His feet as dead. But He laid His right hand on me, saying to me, "Do not be afraid; I am the First and the Last, I am He who lives, and was dead, and behold, I am alive forevermore. Amen. And I have the keys of Hades and of Death." (Revelation 1:17–18)

This is first chapter, and Jesus is victorious and has defeated the devil through His sacrificial death. Jesus is the same yesterday, today, and forever. In Revelation 5, the Spirit revealed to John what it was like when Jesus entered the most holy place in heaven after His resurrection. John was able to see it in the Spirit.

So I wept much, because no one was found worthy to open and read the scroll, or to look at it. But one of the elders said to me, "Do not weep. Behold the Lion of the tribe of Judah, the root of David, has prevailed to open the scroll and to loose its seven seals." And I looked, and behold, in the midst of the throne and the four living creatures, and in the midst of the elders, stood a Lamb as though it had been slain, having seven horns and seven eyes, which are the seven Spirits of God sent out into all the earth. Then He came and took the scroll out of the right hand of Him who sat on the throne. Now when He had taken the scroll, the twenty-four elders fell down before the Lamb, each having a harp,

**and golden bowls full of incense, which
are the prayers of the saints. And they
sang a new song, saying: You are worthy
to take the scroll, and to open its seals;
for you were slain, and have redeemed us
to God by your blood out of every tribe
and tongue and people and nation, and
have made us kings and priests to our
God; and we shall reign on the earth."
(Revelation 5:4–10)**

When I used to read Revelation, I would always think, *I wonder where we are now in terms of the end of the world.* Now I know Jesus revealed Himself to John as a forever-victorious Savior. In Revelation 12:4, it says, "His tail drew a third of the stars of heaven and threw them to the earth. And the dragon stood before the woman who was ready to give birth, to devour her Child as soon as it was born."

This is chapter 12, and the revealing is the birth of Jesus. Jesus is God who became a Man who is and who was and who is to come the Almighty. The Revelation of Jesus Christ is a series of visions given to John in the Spirit realm. The Scripture would not be fulfilled in the future. The fulfillment of that Scripture was in Matthew 2:16–18. Then Herod, when he saw he was deceived by the wise men, was exceedingly angry, and he sent forth and put to death all the male children who were in Bethlehem and in all the districts from two years old and under, according to the time which he had determined from the wise men. Then was fulfilled what was spoken by Jeremiah the prophet, saying, "A voice was heard in Ramah, lamentation, weeping, and great mourning, Rachel weeping for her children, refusing to be comforted, because they are no more."

So the angel thrust his sickle into the earth and gathered the vine of the earth, and threw it into the great winepress of the wrath of God. And the winepress was trampled outside the city, and blood came out of the winepress, up to the horses' bridles, for one thousand six hundred furlongs. (Revelation 14:19–20)

Jesus said, "I am the true vine, and My Father is the vinedresser." Jesus was the vine of the earth, thrown into the great winepress of the wrath of God. In Isaiah 63:2–3, it says, "Why is Your apparel red, and Your garments like one who treads in the winepress? 'I have trodden the winepress alone, and from peoples no one was with Me. For I have trodden them in My anger, and trampled them in My fury; their blood is sprinkled upon My garments, and I have stained all My robes.'" In Hebrews 13:12, it says, "Therefore Jesus also, that He might sanctify the people with His own blood, suffered outside the gate." Jesus' blood in the Spirit was enough to cover the sins of the whole world. This was accomplished at the cross. He who knew no sin became sin that we might become the righteousness of God in Him. It is finished!

The Revelation of Jesus Christ begins in victory, and it ends in victory. He cannot be revealed any other way. He has overcome. Because He lives in you, you also have overcome. God's wrath will continue to be poured out against His enemies. God will not suffer His church to wrath. No evil shall befall you. As He protected the three Hebrew boys, He will protect you. You will not burn, but your adversary will. God is a consuming fire. The same fire that protects and empowers you will consume your adversary. Jesus will come in His glorified body at the set time. Until then, you are His body, operating in the earth realm. The same Spirit that raised Jesus from the dead now dwells in your mortal body—the Lord, who is and was and is to come, the Almighty. Some things are still to come. The devil and death and hades will be cast into the lake of fire, but that will not affect your glorious lifestyle in God.

Decrees

- As He is, so am I in this world.
- I decree a victory mentality in the church of Jesus Christ.
- No weapon formed against you shall prosper.
- Every tongue that rises against you in judgment, condemn it.
- It is finished!
- I decree that souls come out of darkness and into your marvelous light.
- It is done.

CHAPTER 16

The Liberation of the Earth

The liberation of the earth has been going on for two thousand years. There has been a constant increase in light since the outpouring of the Spirit of Jesus on the day of Pentecost. The devil knows he is defeated, so he attempts to suppress the truth of the victory of Jesus Christ. God told Adam, "Cursed is the ground for your sake." From the dust you are, and to the dust you shall return. The last enemy that will be destroyed is death. Jesus destroyed that enemy in the eternal realm two thousand years ago. For the things that can be seen with the natural eye are temporary. They are still aging and dying, but there is an unseen realm that is eternal. That which you cannot see is eternal.

I was still on drugs in November 1978. I loved my grandpa (Pap) as much as anyone on earth. But five years of daily drug use had really hardened my heart toward loving anyone, including Pap. My grandmother called and said Pap wanted me to come down and talk to him. He lived about ten miles away. I drove down to see him. He was really sick with emphysema. He was on the couch, lying down. He said, "Sit down, son."

I sat at his feet on the couch.

He said, "Son, I want you to make me a promise."

I said, "What do you need?"

He said, "Promise you will give your life to Jesus Christ."

I said, "Pap, I believe in Jesus."

He said, "You may believe in Him, but you have never given your life to Him. Promise me you will because, son, I want to see you again. And where I am going and where you are going is not the same place. Son, I am dying, and I want to see you again."

I said, "Pap, you're not dying."

He said, "Son, I am. Promise you will give your life to Jesus."

I promised him that I would. He did pass away the next week, on November 11, 1978. The family was all standing around his bed, and the last words he spoke to all of us was, believe in God.

My grandma (Mam) and Pap were in a one-room school together in the early 1900s. He was nine years old, and she was four. Pap ran up to her at recess one day and said, "Ruby (Mam), I'm going to marry you some day." About fifteen years later, they did get married. Mam was one of the strongest people I have ever known. But the night Pap died, she kind of collapsed in another bedroom. I said, "Mam, you will be all right. Pap is in heaven."

She said, "You don't understand. He was my life. I have never known life without him. I cannot live another day without him."

For the next months, I would drive down to her house and eat supper once a week. One night, after about two months, she was different. She seemed much better. I said, "Mam, you are different. What happened?"

She said, "Nothing happened."

I said, "Mam, something happened. You are different."

She said, "You will think I'm crazy. A few nights ago, I was sitting here on the couch, and I looked up, and Pap was standing right here in front of me. He said, 'Ruby, quit grieving. I am alive, and everything is fine."

I said, "What happened then?"

She said, "He just went right up through the ceiling."

Mam lived thirty-two more years after seeing Pap. She knew he was alive, and the reunion was certain. By the way, I did get saved on March 25, 1979. Praise God!

Pap never saw death. His body is still in the ground at Bond's Chapel Cemetery, but he was never one second out of life. Jesus said, "He who lives and believes in Me will never die." Do you believe this?

The earth is the Lord's and the fullness thereof. Death will be destroyed in the seen (temporary) realm. Mortality will be swallowed up by life. The Revelation of Jesus Christ is the series of visions shown to John in the Spirit. It revealed everything that was accomplished in the eternal spirit realm by Jesus Christ's birth, death, and resurrection. The battle of Armageddon was fought and won against the kings (fallen angels) and the devil himself in the Spirit. Jesus' body was dead three days. His soul was made a sin offering. His soul was dead because of sin. He who knew no sin became sin. When the Spirit of God entered His dead soul that had been offered for sin, the new creation started. Jesus made a public spectacle of the fallen angels, triumphing over them. This was all in the Spirit. Jesus is alive and forever victorious. Jesus is on the throne of God. The devil and all the fallen angels are forever defeated in the spirit realm forever.

The eyes of your understanding being enlightened; that you may know what is the hope of His calling, what are the riches of the glory of His inheritance in the saints, and what is the exceeding greatness of His power toward us

**who believe, according to the working
of His mighty power which He worked
in Christ when He raised Him from the
dead and seated Him at His right hand
in the heavenly places, far above all
principality and power and dominion,
and every name that is named, not only
in this age but also in that which is to
come. And He put all things under His
feet, and gave Him to be head over all
things to the church, which is His body,
the fullness of Him who fills all in all.
(Ephesians 1:18–23)**

Jesus is the head of the church. Jesus is God on the throne as a man in His glorified human body. We are His body on the earth. Jesus is at the right hand of the Father until His enemies are made His footstool. The body of Jesus is one body. Jesus will use men with His Spirit to make His enemies His footstool. The battle between the angels and Man is over in the Spirit. Jesus won! Jesus, the Man, is on the throne of God.

The devil and his angels are forever defeated by the death and resurrection of Jesus. The devil is the head of the fallen angels. The devil uses the bodies of men and women to carry out his schemes. The battle being waged now between Jesus Christ and the devil is not a military battle being fought in the natural. These are wars contrived by evil men, knowingly being used by fallen angels.

For the mystery of lawlessness is already at work; only he who now restrains will do so until he is taken out of the way. (2 Thessalonians 2:7)

If the *He* in the above scripture is God, then that would be rapture. The church and the Spirit are removed. If the *he* is the spirit of antichrist operating through men, it would mean dominion for Man and the defeat of the Lord's enemies. The devil and his angels are using men to restrain and suppress the truth that Jesus Christ has overcome, and Man has dominion of the earth once again and forevermore. The kingdom of God is the righteous government on the earth, and the body of Jesus cannot be defeated. As the sons of God are being revealed, the sons of the devil are also being revealed. As Jesus uses His body (believers), the devil uses his body, which is men, suppressing the truth of the gospel. Just a few years ago, a sitting president was censored from Facebook and Twitter. It seems like the body of sin, the man of sin, is advancing. It actually is the opposite.

As the light of God grows stronger in His body on earth, the darkness is exposed to be destroyed.

> **Till we all come to the unity of the faith and of the knowledge of the Son of God, to a perfect man, to the measure of the stature of the fullness of Christ. (Ephesians 4:13)**

The devil is manifesting in his body through school shootings, the state taking authority for children having sex changes and puberty blockers without the parents' permission. The fallen angels through district attorneys are mandating lawlessness in cities and influencing corporations to promote sexual perversion in clothing (Target). The fallen angels are using politicians to kill babies at all costs.

Jesus is saying to His body on earth, "I want you to know that I am alive in you. I want you to know you have a new identity. I want you to know that the One who defeated the devil and death is in your mortal body. When you fully agree that is not you who lives anymore but Jesus Christ in you, then you will begin to manifest My magnificent glory. You are My body. You are the light of the world. You are the city set on a hill. Greater things than I performed, you will perform because My Father and I are in you, and you are 2.6 billion strong." I pray a quickening in the body of Jesus to be filled (baptized) with His Spirit. I was saved twelve years without the baptism of His Spirit. I was going to heaven, but I did not have power. The power of miracles is in the baptism of the Spirit. It is then the rivers of living water, flowing out of your heart, producing miracles. You will pray in tongues, but that is a witness. The baptism of the Spirit is all about power—power to destroy the lying fallen angels in the name of Jesus. Jesus is the Spirit of God in the new covenant. Ask him to baptize you now and receive His resurrected power. I have prayed in the Spirit every day since 1991. Pray in the Spirit, and pray with understanding also. To have tongues and then not pray in tongues does you no good. Desire to prophesy. Build up others in the faith. We are one body.

The first commandment in the New Testament is to love the Lord with all your heart, with all your soul, with all your strength, and with all your mind. Your love for Father and Jesus must be first. It is your love for God that opens all doors to the supernatural. Faith and obedience must be in place for God's power to flow. Praise and thanksgiving to God for His goodness must be a way of life. This is the love of God, not that we love God but that He loves us and gave His Son for the payment for all our sins.

As faith and understanding come concerning your new identity, you will begin to manifest miracles, signs, wonders, and supernatural abundance for every good work. The battle being waged now on earth is between the body of a Man (Jesus) and the body of a fallen angel (man of sin). The man of sin is a collective body of men, suppressing the truth.

As the light and revelation of Jesus increases in His body, the restraints of evil men and defeated fallen angels will be taken out of the way. The glorious light of the body of Jesus (church) on the earth will remove all suppressing of the truth. The church will so magnify in the revelation of Jesus Christ that even the last enemy will be destroyed (death).

The Revelation of Jesus Christ is not in chronological order; it is a series of visions given to John in the Spirit. It is not the revelation of end-times. Jesus is eternally victorious in the Spirit. Second Thessalonians 2:7–8 is in chronological order. After the men and the fallen angels that are restraining the truth are taken out of the way (by the decrees of the church), then the lawless one will be revealed, whom the Lord will consume with the breath of His mouth and destroy with the brightness of His coming. God is a consuming fire.

The earth is about to be fully liberated by the sons of God. The kingdom of God has come. Dominion has been restored to Man. Heaven and earth are one. All of creation will cry out Hosanna. Everything is controlled by God again. Salvation and glory and honor and power belong to the Lord, our God!

Decrees

- I decree that souls come out of darkness and into Jesus' marvelous light.
- Do not be weary in well doing; you will reap if you do not faint.
- And this is the love of God, that He loves us and gave His life for us.
- Glory be to the name of Jesus forever and ever!
- The earth will be filled with the knowledge of the glory of the Lord as the waters cover the sea.
- The best is yet to come. All glory to Jesus.
- Selah.

ABOUT THE AUTHOR

With more than thirty years in the pul-
pit, Dwight Dunbar is a leading voice
in proclaiming the gospel in Southern
Indiana through radio and television
ministries. Pastor Dunbar founded
Work of God Inc. in 2000. Pastor
Dunbar has transitioned from being

active in the marketplace in November 2021, where he was
involved in several businesses. He has also served on the
board of directors for the Lawrence County Community
Foundation and has served as a director of the Mitchell
Chamber of Commerce. Pastor Dunbar has been married
to his wife, Kathy, for over forty years. Dwight and Kathy
have two children and three grandchildren.

www.ingramcontent.com/pod-product-compliance
Lightning Source LLC
Chambersburg PA
CBHW031415150726
47989CB00002B/669